3

Studies informing the Framework for the Assessment of Children in Need and their Families

Department of Health

Janet Seden

Ruth Sinclair

Diana Robbins

Clare Pont

London: The Stationery Office

D0294323

Cover photograph supplied courtesy of www.JohnBirdsall.co.uk

First published 2001
Second impression 2002

ISBN 0 11 322302 1

Published by The Stationery Office and available from:

The Stationery Office
(mail, telephone and fax orders only)
PO Box 29, Norwich NR3 1GN
Telephone orders/General enquiries 0870 600 5522
Fax orders 0870 600 5533

www.thestationeryoffice.com

The Stationery Office Bookshops
123 Kingsway, London WC2B 6PQ
020 7242 6393 Fax 020 7242 6394
68–69 Bull Street, Birmingham B4 6AD
0121 236 9696 Fax 0121 236 9699
33 Wine Street, Bristol BS1 2BQ
0117 926 4306 Fax 0117 929 4515
9–21 Princess Street, Manchester M60 8AS
0161 834 7201 Fax 0161 833 0634
16 Arthur Street, Belfast BT1 4GD
028 9023 8451 Fax 028 9023 5401
The Stationery Office Oriel Bookshop
18–19 High Street, Cardiff CF1 2BZ
029 2039 5548 Fax 029 2038 4347
71 Lothian Road, Edinburgh EH3 9AZ
0870 606 5566 Fax 0870 606 5588

The Stationery Office's Accredited Agents
(see Yellow Pages)

and through good booksellers

Printed in the United Kingdom for The Stationery Office
689782   1/02   C20   019585

Contents

Introduction

The *Framework for the Assessment of Children in Need and their Families* (Department of Health et al, 2000) was published in April 2000. It provides a systematic way of analysing, understanding and recording what is happening to children and young people within their families and the wider context of the community in which they live. From such an understanding of what are inevitably complex issues and inter-relationships, clear professional judgements can be made. These judgements include whether the child being assessed is in need, whether the child is suffering or likely to suffer significant harm, what actions must be taken and which services would best meet the needs of this particular child and family. The evidence based knowledge which has informed the development of the Assessment Framework has been drawn from a wide range of research studies and theories across a number of disciplines and from the accumulated experience of policy and practice.

The four studies in this publication provided part of that evidence base and were undertaken to inform the development of the Assessment Framework. Their key messages were also incorporated into the training materials *The Child's World: Assessing Children in Need* (NSPCC and University of Sheffield, 2000) published to support the implementation of the Assessment Framework.

Janet Seden undertook a review of social work literature on assessment. This work made a significant contribution to the theoretical basis of the Assessment Framework. It provided a baseline from which to proceed and identified areas requiring further work. In particular, it identified that the theory of social work practice requires updating to take account of developments in practice over the past twenty years.

The *Framework for the Assessment of Children in Need and their Families* is intended to assist practitioners and their managers ascertain with the family whether a child is in need and how that child and family might best be helped. An assessment of a child's needs is a critical task. Research findings (Department of Health, 1995b) had previously indicated that children's needs were all too often expressed in terms of services children required rather than their developmental needs. In order to review current practice, a study of the language used by social workers to describe the needs of children was undertaken by Ruth Sinclair and the Social Services Inspectorate. A key finding was that where the Looking After Children materials (Department of Health, 1995a) were being used by social workers, they were describing the needs of children according to the seven child developmental dimensions of that programme. This information was particularly helpful when considering the training needs of practitioners and their managers.

The development of the Assessment Framework began as a number of changes were being debated about the way in which the public sector is organised and responsibilities allocated. In order to inform the Department of Health's deliberations a study of different structures and types of assessments was undertaken in a variety of settings. The field work was undertaken by the Social Services Inspectorate and the findings written up by Diana Robbins. Within the settings studied, assessments were being undertaken by staff employed by social services departments, the NHS and voluntary agencies and staff worked across a continuum from single agency assessment to multi-disciplinary, multi-agency team work. The conclusions drawn from the study suggest the type of settings, structures and cultures that facilitate assessment work.

In the fourth study, Clare Pont summarises the findings about assessment from child care inspections undertaken by the Social Services Inspectorate, Department of Health during the period 1993-1997. Her report identifies key messages for practitioners, managers and policy makers in relation to assessment. These lessons were incorporated into the Assessment Framework and informed *The Child's World* development and training pack.

These four studies provide a valuable source of information about practice and thinking at the time the Assessment Framework was being developed. The intention is that they will inform the field, and assist in understanding the background and principles underpinning the Assessment Framework. Managers and trainers will find the studies provide valuable material for training programmes on the Assessment Framework and issues raised which should be considered in planning the implementation of the Framework.

Finally, these studies constitute important baseline information for the subsequent review and evaluation of the impact of the Assessment Framework.

Jenny Gray
Children's Services Branch
Social Care Group
Department of Health

REFERENCES

Department of Health (1995a) *Looking After Children*. HMSO, London.

Department of Health (1995b) *Child Protection: Messages from Research*. HMSO, London.

Department of Health, Department for Education and Employment and Home Office (2000) *Framework for the Assessment of Children in Need and their Families*. The Stationery Office, London.

The NSPCC and the University of Sheffield (2000) *The Child's World: Assessing Children in Need. Training and Development Pack*. The NSPCC, London.

Study A

Assessment of children in need and their families: a literature review

Janet Seden

Study A: Contents

Acknowledgements

It has been a pleasure and a privilege to have had the opportunity to undertake the research which has resulted in this literature review for the Department of Health. Thanks are due to Jenny Gray for commissioning the project, and to her team of advisors, including Margaret Adcock, for their advice and support. As ever, I am indebted to Professor Jane Aldgate, and also to Wendy Rose and Hedy Cleaver, who have 'advised, assisted and befriended' throughout. I would also like to thank Chris Cazalet for her patience and flexibility throughout the many edits.

Janet Seden
December 2000

Introduction

This review has contributed to the development of the **Framework for the Assessment of Children in Need and their Families** (Department of Health et al, 2000) by identifying and evaluating the efficacy of key models for assessing children and families which are currently in use or being developed. It identifies and evaluates their use for different levels and types of assessments, explores their theoretical bases and evaluates their strengths and weaknesses. The impact of race, culture, gender, language and disability have been considered throughout.

Additionally, the review identifies and documents which human development theories can be drawn on to complement the child development theoretical underpinnings of the Assessment Framework. Such findings from literature enhance the practitioner's understanding of the relationship between the selected model and the purpose of the assessment, as well the relationship between the planned interventions and the desired outcomes for children and their families.

The review began by searching academic journals and texts relating to social care, probation, prison and health care services as well as aspects of employment, economics, politics, sociology and race relations. Some texts were selected for more detailed review because they were well established in teaching and practice, or because they were recent compilations of research and practice. In addition, contact was made with some voluntary children's services to request published or unpublished models and frameworks for assessment which they had found helpful.

The literature which is cited draws on a wide range of professional disciplines, and includes international sources. Conceptual frameworks or research from other countries, however, should be understood in the context in which they were developed before evaluating their relevance to England. For example, both the USA and Australia are engaged in similar debates about the provision of children's services but their legal and operational contexts differ from England (Maluccio, 1997; Victoria Youth and Family Services, Service Delivery Document, 1997).

The results of this review uncovered an extensive literature about the assessment of children and families which merits continued examination. It also identified areas in which further development of the theoretical bases to practice would make a significant contribution to modernising the nature of work with children in need and their families.

1 The Development of Assessment in Social Work

Introduction

Assessment in children's services is the foundation of planning and decision making (Adcock and White, 1998). It is a cornerstone of professional activity in health, education, voluntary sector provision, social services, housing, benefits agencies and other services which are available to children and their families. It can be argued that the key components of an assessment framework in children's and family work are that the framework is:

- underpinned by knowledge from research, literature and practice

- evidence based, particularly related to child development, family functioning and the environment in which children grow up

- built on concepts of need which are relevant, holistic and child centred

- congruent with the principles of relevant legislation

- explicit about the theories, models and methods used

- capable of being developed and evaluated.

Generally, social work activity comprises cycles of assessment, intervention and evaluation in which goals are identified, actions taken and resources mobilised. These cycles take place within legal, organisational and ethical boundaries. Assessment is the first stage of a process aimed at achieving specified outcomes and not, as sometimes has become in practice, an end in itself. It is also important to understand that the process of assessment may contribute to the achievement of outcomes by the way it is undertaken.

The origins of social work assessment

Early writing on casework borrowed from medicine and constructed the concept of 'social diagnosis' (Richmond, 1922; Hollis, 1964). This model for assessment, which concentrated on an individual's dysfunction, remained in general use until the early 1970s. Increasingly, however, there began to emerge a recognition that individuals were influenced by their social circumstances. John Haines (1975 p. 16) describes social work assessment as 'the ability to assess a social situation and intervene in whatever seems to be the most effective way'. He conceptualises the social work process as 'assessment, action and evaluation' in which the purpose of assessment is:

> To gather as much information as possible about the situation and form some opinion about its meaning for the client and its implications for action.

Haines' work was taken further in the late 1970s by Curnock and Hardiker (1979). Assessment is conceptualised by these authors as a filter by which practitioners weigh and sift information in order to plan their interventions. They describe the stages of assessment as:

- acquisition of information

- studying facts and feelings

- balancing and formulating

- strategies in goal setting

- intervention.

Curnock and Hardiker's (1979 p. 162) model of assessment is constructed from purposive empirical research with practitioners in probation, child care and mental health settings, thus conceptualising from practice that which has been observed and analysed. They also usefully define the elements of assessment as:

- frameworks

- communication

- balance sheets of risks, needs and resources

- goal setting strategies.

They suggest that the phases overlap and that assessment is not a static process. Assessment is informed by paradigms (or theory frameworks) which guide the practitioner. Compton and Galaway (1989) develop further the concept of assessment through their classic text, *Social Work Processes,* which makes a major contribution to social work theory and practice. They suggest that, 'the ultimate purpose of assessment is to contribute the understanding necessary for appropriate planning' (p. 414). The phases of assessment are described as (pp. 452-454):

- purpose and process

- doing the assessment

- exploring the problem

- putting meaning to the situation

- feelings and facts.

Similar assessment frameworks have been developed by Pincus and Minahan, 1973; Specht and Vickery, 1977; Coulshed, 1991; Meyer, 1993. These are widely cited in social work literature and continue to be applied to a range of tasks (Taylor and Devine, 1993; Thompson, 1995; Sinclair et al. 1995). These frameworks are essentially about ways in which practitioners interact with the public to gather relevant information and formulate ways of achieving specified outcomes.

However, while the principle of undertaking assessment has been well established, the purposes and theory bases have developed in different directions. The main shift in the ideology of assessment since 1970 has been a move away from a diagnostic focus towards understanding the perspectives of the service user within a holistic and person centred framework (White and Epston, 1990; Meyer, 1993; Lloyd and Taylor, 1995). These approaches build on the identified strengths of individuals rather than looking for dysfunction. They emphasise assessing what is present in terms of the service user's strengths to establish successful ways of problem solving (de Schazer, 1985). In some models, the service users' narratives or stories determine the process (Franklin and Jordan, 1995; Laird, 1995).

This body of work shows that there is a spectrum of models of assessment from diagnosis of dysfunction through problem solving to the designation of service users as 'expert' about their own situation. The existence of different approaches, each with their own advocates, sets up a tension between diagnostic (exclusion/pathology) and social (inclusion/strengths) approaches to assessment which may be spurious. In practice, the use of different approaches may relate more to the context of assessment and its purpose rather than the framework per se. This tension has manifested itself in two predominating approaches; risk assessment and empowerment.

The preoccupation with risk assessment

So far, there has been discussion about the emergence of different approaches to assessment which have been applied generally to social work activity. However, in relation to assessing children and their families, there has been a preoccupation over the last twenty years with models for risk assessment which have tended to stress family dysfunction rather than strengths. This is understandable as, since the death of Maria Colwell in 1973, the public anxiety about preventing child deaths has permeated practitioners' perceptions of their role in a fundamental way. Highly publicised 'failures' to protect children from danger have led the professions to develop checklists of indicators and predictors which claim to measure the safety of a child within a family. Consequently, much of the literature has been about the development of scales to assess the risks to children from parental dangerousness (Kempshall, 1995; Prins, 1995; Home Office, 1997).

To some extent, this approach has been justified by evidence from research. Children's wellbeing may be affected in certain circumstances by the behaviour of parents who use alcohol and other substances (Sheridan, 1995; Azzi-Lessing and Allen, 1996; Cleaver et al. 1999); suffer mental illness (Sheppard, 1993) and are violent in the home (Farmer and Owen, 1995; Brandon et al. 1996; Hemming et al. 1997; Kaufman and Jasinski, 1997). However, the research urges caution on the part of practitioners as there is still no fail-safe way of predicting which child will suffer, or is likely to suffer, serious harm.

Risk assessment scales, at their present stage of development and implementation, offer a range of predictors and factors derived from what in the past has contributed to dangerous actions. They provide a map of clusters of factors which, when aggregated, indicate cause for concern. The deficit of this approach is that, despite increasing sophistication in the ability to devise scales and evaluate them, the variables involved and their inter-relationships are so complex that any decision making requires a high level of professional judgement and qualitative assessment. There is literature to assist with this decision making (Schon, 1983; Dowie and Elstein, 1988; Schaffer, 1990; Lindsey, 1994; Yelloly and Henkel, 1995).

Re-visiting risk assessment

Recently, literature has indicated the beginnings of some disaffection with a risk assessment approach because of the problem of making sense of undifferentiated data (Wald and Woolverton, 1990; English and Pecora, 1994; Corby, 1996).

Lyons, Wodarski and Doueck (1996) review ten risk assessment models and their usefulness. They appear to endorse the caution sounded by Corby, concluding that further development of models is needed. Likewise Gaudin et al. (1992) conclude that models for risk assessment are still not developed enough to be more than useful in guiding the management of individual cases. Corby (1996, p. 27) concludes:

> Considerable attention has been paid to the context in which child protection assessments are carried out at both macro and micro levels. It has been emphasised that at the macro level there is still great uncertainty about the extent to which the state should intervene in families to protect children. This is a value laden issue that will not be resolved by the development of more scientific approaches to risk assessment. At the micro level, perhaps because of societal ambivalence, there are many barriers to conducting assessments as nationally and comprehensively as many professionals would like.

The literature from the USA has identified another set of problems of risk assessment: inadequate implementation and difficulties in evaluation (Doueck et al. 1992; Murphy-Berman, 1994). Risk assessment procedures are seen to vary on a number of dimensions, are complex to compare against each other, and need to take account of variables such as the purpose of the assessment and the nature of the decisions to be made.

The Australian picture is similar. A study in 1989 concludes that risk indicators provide a framework for assessment which can eliminate much idiosyncratic decision making but that no indicators can be 'perfect predictors' or capture the whole (Dalgleish and Drew, 1989 p. 500). Dalgleish (1997, 1999) takes this work forward by evaluating eight risk assessment models and developing a new model which separates the analysis of risk from the judgement about what is an acceptable degree of risk and subsequent decision making. The experience, expectations, motivations and history of the social worker are considered to 'make explicit aspects of the judgements and decisions made by child protection workers in uncertain and risky situations'. This work is a valuable contribution to clarifying the issues of implementation and training for professionals using risk assessment scales because it considers carefully the contribution of the complex contexts which affect professional decision making.

As Jones (1997, p. 522) writes in relation to child abuse 'in short once maltreatment has taken place, and before we can consider the possible outcomes for the child, we need to take into account a range of intervening variables'. The complexity of aggregating the range of factors identified in risk assessment cases and the care which has to be taken to decide which framework to use for what purpose is delineated by Hagell (1998) who considers a diverse and sometimes conflicting literature. The review is an excellent and comprehensive analysis which reinforces the difficulties of practice applications in relation to assessing 'dangerous parenting'.

In conclusion, it can be said that checklists are helpful mapping tools in decision making but they cannot be used without professional judgement. The literature shows how reasoned and balanced professional judgements carefully made by those with 'quality' and skill remain crucial. The strengths of risk assessment scales are in providing a rational framework for the collation of data which identifies dangerousness. The deficits are that, despite increasing sophistication in the design and evaluation of risk assessment tools, the variables for assessing children in the contexts of their families are so complex that professional judgement underpinned by theory and research still remains the cornerstone of best practice.

The developing importance of empowerment

The concept of empowerment emerged in social work through writing such as that of Solomon in relation to black communities in the USA (Solomon, 1976). Empowerment has since become a dominant theme in contemporary social work literature and practice, reflecting a concern with the social inequalities and social exclusion faced by many of the client groups with whom practitioners work. It is important that strategies for empowerment remain driven by this genuine concern to redress inequalities, based on knowledge from empirical research, and do not become mere tokenism (Humphries, 1996).

Empowerment in social work practice is complex because it encompasses values, ideology and methods. It has been argued that (Payne, 1992, p. 229) an 'empowerment strategy requires commitment to both maintenance and improvement of effective equal services and also to confrontation of pervasive negative valuations'. The aims of empowerment are to help service users see (1992, p. 230):

- themselves as causal agents in finding solutions to their problems;

- social workers as having knowledge and skills that service users can use;

- social workers as peers and partners in solving problems;

- the power structure as complex and partly open to influence.

This leads to a model of practice which enables individuals to see themselves as having some control over their situation. The social worker's role becomes that of 'resources consultant, sensitiser and trainer' (Payne, 1992, p. 230).

Empowerment is an ideological stance in assessment work with children and families which claims to counteract negative self-evaluations, deriving from oppression or disadvantage. While in some types of social work, ideas of empowerment may have led to a rigid approach, in others it has resulted in the development of innovative ways of working in partnership with families. Empowerment at its best is a positive outcome of actions undertaken by social worker, child, family and necessary others working together.

In practice, there are examples of how this has been achieved. For example, family centres in the voluntary sector and some local authority specialist services have been developing an approach to assessment which, based on ideas of empowerment, is designed to strengthen and support families to achieve their goals. These approaches aim to work closely with parents, carers and children on a partnership model. They include the development of assessment tools which can be shared with and understood by everyone concerned in the assessment process.

There is a range of practice accounts of the partnership approach (eg. Whalley, 1994; Weick and Saleeby, 1995; Scott and O'Neill, 1996; Scannapieco and Hegar, 1996). Five interesting examples of practice materials which the reader may care to consider are:

The NSPCC in association with Chailey Heritage and with the support of the the Department of Health (1997) developed the training pack **Turning Points: A Resource Pack for Communicating with Children** which offers models for communicating with children on which practitioners can draw. The materials are designed for use by professionals who wish to improve their communication skills with children. The aim is to provide a resource to raise the standards of communication with children, reduce barriers and help practitioners to enable children to:

- express their wishes and feelings;

- make sense of their circumstances;

- participate more fully on decisions which affect them.

This publication is intended for use by all professionals working with children and is underpinned by child development knowledge from a range of disciplines.

The NCH Action for Children **Practice Guidelines** (1996) is a comprehensive policy and practice document compiled for trained personnel working with children and young people who abuse others. It contains practice guidelines, references for further reading and information about contacts for consultancy and training. It includes an assessment schedule detailing, under four headings, the information required. Each essential component being assessed is specified and then considered under the headings:

- What do we need to know?

- How do we obtain the relevant information?

- What are the tools?

- What are the issues that require attention?

This takes the practitioner through an orderly but open-ended process, drawing attention not only to the critical issues and the information required (in detail) but also leads them to think about how to communicate effectively with children and families.

The National Council for Voluntary Child Care Organisations, publication, **Finding Out**, (Van der Eyken et al., 1997) is designed to be used in family centres to evaluate the effectiveness of the work with families. It contains innovatively designed questionnaires which aim to develop a flexible, creative and constructive framework for asking questions, especially of children. The tools to be used with children and parents are beautifully designed and presented. There are examples of schedules which can help workers in their direct work with children and their families.

The NCH Action for Children's Assessing **Younger Children and Families, Whale by the Tail** (Gaffney, 1998) is specially designed for use with children aged under five and their families. It contains a comprehensive set of questionnaires to help workers and families plan together for change. While knowledge, skills and experience will inform judgements, the methodology keeps children in mind and provides a range of tools to explore areas such as children's issues, parenting issues, attachment, confidence and relationships. A similarly useful pack, yet unpublished, is being implemented at another NCH family centre (Holt, 1998).

Concurrent Planning (Katz et al., 1994) offers clear assessment tools, which will be easily understood by families. A particular strength of this material is the system of summaries of relevant theoretical underpinnings for the schedules, from attachment and other child development knowledge, set out in a clear and accessible format. It is very well referenced to relevant research and writing. While this is designed for assessment in the adoption context, the methods could be adapted to work with children in the community.

Alongside these five examples, there are other relevant accounts of working in different circumstances from empowerment principles. Particularly useful are the approaches demonstrated by Thoburn et al. (1995) and Brandon et al. (1999) which show that even in cases where severe maltreatment is suspected, or has occurred, a partnership approach can be beneficial to improve parenting capacity.

Therefore, while there must be questions raised about partnership approaches if they are ideologically driven and rigidly applied, on balance they can be seen to have some considerable advantages. Partnership which builds on family strengths, offers assessment tools which involve children and families in the social work process and takes account of their perspectives can produce empowering outcomes. There is substantial evidence from literature and recent research into social work practice with children and their families that working in this way can result in the empowerment of children and their parents to enable them to manage their difficulties more positively, developing increased self-esteem and self-efficacy.

2 *Underpinning Psychological Theories*

…to practice without theory is to sail an uncharted sea; theory without practice is not to sail at all…

(Susser quoted in Hardiker and Barker, 1991, p. 87)

Introduction

The previous chapter explored the development of different approaches to assessment in social work. These approaches are derived from a knowledge base which is multi-faceted. Hardiker and Barker (1991, p. 87) suggest that social work:

requires a breadth of discipline knowledge (eg. law, psychiatry and philosophy). Furthermore, social workers need to be sufficiently familiar with them to make informed choices, keep up to date with advances and to discard redundant theories.

This chapter discusses the underpinning theories for assessment and intervention in social work practice and some of the methods that derive from them.

An eclectic approach to theory

In order to fulfil their tasks, social workers have drawn from other disciplines including:

- sociology, to understand the social construction of problems in society;

- psychology, to understand individual and group functioning;

- social policy, to understand the structural factors which affect individuals.

It can be argued that social work has been unnecessarily apologetic about this, as the strength of social work's eclectic history has made for a versatile response to the requirement to operate in diverse legal and bureaucratic frameworks. Advantages of the eclectic approach when it is thoughtful and disciplined are:

- the merging of theories for the benefit of the service user, thus enabling a customised approach;

- avoidance of the narrow dogmatism which can accompany a one-theory approach;

- the ability to be flexible and adapt to changing social policy and social conditions;

- the ability to work with other professionals from overlapping theoretical bases.

No new grand theories have emerged to underpin social work practice in the last two decades, either nationally or internationally, but the application of theory in practice has been modified over time. Those approaches which are commonly found in the core texts for practice (Compton and Galaway, 1989; Howe, 1987; Coulshed, 1991; Lishman, 1991; Payne, 1992) have been subject to re-definition and re-evaluation as social attitudes, values and beliefs change. They have particularly been re-examined for usefulness in relation to changes in legislation and the policies which guide practice (the Children Act 1989, the NHS and Community Care Act 1990, the Criminal Justice Act 1991). Social workers have proved resourceful in adapting their tried methods to new legislative expectations (Hardiker and Barker, 1994, 1996; Marsh and Triseliotis, 1996).

Selected theories relevant for practice

Having set assessment in the context of differing theoretical approaches, there are some key psychological theories which deserve closer attention. These are reviewed and their application to practice considered in the following section.

Psychodynamic theory

History

Psychodynamic practice was integrated into social work in the United Kingdom from America and became established in the 1950s, 1960s and 1970s. The ideas it espouses about how personality is formed and developed derive from Freudian psycho-analysis. Social work utilises psychodynamic insights for ways of understanding relationships, such as self and significant others; past and present experience; and inner and outer experience. It is sometimes wrongly confused with the psychosocial approach. The psychosocial model derives many concepts from psychodynamic theory and ego psychology but combines the personal, the social and the practical into a more holistic framework (ie. social casework). A strictly psychodynamic approach, as practised in some counselling, only considers the external world from the service user's view. It is, therefore, on rare occasions that a purely psychodynamic approach is used by social workers. Research studies have showed that few service users benefit from its indiscriminate use (Mayer and Timms, 1970). Its strengths are that it has been highly influential in providing social workers with ways of understanding those they work with. Furthermore, the important idea of the use of the relationship as an agent of change, which permeates social work practice, is essentially a psychodynamic one.

Current practice

Pyschodynamic ideas are particularly relevant in children and families social work because of their influence in studies of human development (Fairbairn, 1952; Erikson, 1965; Winnicott, 1986; Bowlby, 1988; Rutter et al., 1994). The place of psychodynamic thinking in social work is explored in a number of texts (Yelloly, 1980; Pearson et al., 1988; Brearley, 1991). It underpins at a very fundamental level both past and current research and practice in relation to children and families. Trowell and Bower (1996) have produced a useful reader illustrating the ways in which psycho-analytic ideas can be used in social services, hospitals, schools and community settings to help children. This book is well informed, practical and current, providing both practical examples and theoretical insights. Psycho-analytical ideas have also been applied in the literature on professional supervision (Hawkins and Shohet, 1989; Kadushin, 1997).

In summary

The strengths of the psychodynamic approach for assessment are its usefulness as a way of:

- understanding people;

- assessing the impact of past on present;

- building relationships with people to achieve change;

- understanding children and their behaviours;

- understanding and working with hostility, loss, change, transition, bereavement, defensiveness;

- providing tools for relationship building (derivative counselling skills);

- understanding groups and how they function.

The weaknesses of the approach for assessment are the potential for:

- failing to take account of the external environment;

- pathologising and seeing weaknesses rather than strengths;

- misunderstandings unless the re-evaluations of Freudian theory on women and sexuality are taken into account.

One of the main problems with the psychodynamic approach has been the difficulty of measuring its effectiveness. However, psychodynamic theories offer social workers one way of understanding and interpreting human behaviour (Brearley, 1991). It can be argued that the current 'unfashionableness' of the approach on some social work programmes has deprived practitioners of a useful theoretical base.

Learning theory

History

Behavioural social work, behavioural therapy and behaviour modification derive from learning theory. As Hudson (1991, p. 123) states:

> Learning theories form a body of theory about how behaviour changes as a result of experience, how behaviour is learned, maintained and unlearned.

Learning theory is based on scientific experiments and is consistently modified on the basis of new findings. Its origins come from classical experiments on animals, for example the work by Pavlov and Skinner, and from work with children by Watson and Rayner (all described in some detail by Hudson, 1991).

Current practice

Behavioural social work begins with an assessment to establish a base line from which to plan goals for change. Behaviours are analysed and intervention techniques based on operant learning, respondent conditioning; social learning methods are then used as the tools for intervention. Evaluation of outcome is made against the initial base line. There are full discussions in several key texts (Sheldon, 1982; Hudson and MacDonald, 1986; Howe, 1987; Coulshed, 1991; Payne, 1992). A major strand of the literature is concerned with children. Hudson and MacDonald (1986) outline a range of possible applications, including: anger control and child management with parents who abuse; helping foster carers manage children's behaviour; use in residential settings.

In summary

The strength of the approach for assessment is that:

● it avoids labelling because it focuses on specific observable behaviours: eg not 'he is aggressive and disobedient' (labelling) but he 'hits other children when he loses a game' (specific);

● it gives a baseline for measuring change and evaluating the efficacy of interventions;

- it is a key and crucial perspective in assessing child and parent interactions in a specific and focused framework which can be linked to outcomes.

The questions about behavioural social work are less concerned with its efficacy and more with the ethics and issues of social control. Herbert has a range of detailed assessment schedules and interventions which avoid mystifying jargon. They are applicable for practitioners working with children, young people and their families (Herbert, 1981; 1987; 1989; 1997).

Cognitive-behavioural social work

Cognitive understandings have been increasingly integrated with behavioural practice in the late 1980s and 1990s. This development has proved significant in providing focused frameworks for practitioners to use. These cognitive-behavioural approaches seek to modify the conclusions people draw from their experiences and the consequent maladaptive behaviours. Practitioner emphasis is on reinforcing positive behaviour and thinking, using contracts and activity-based, problem solving tasks. A cognitive approach aims, as Sheldon (1995, p. 214) shows, to modify:

- negatively selective self-perceptions;

- irrational thoughts and thinking styles;

- self-talk and internal dialogue;

- catastrophic imagery associated with particular behaviours and settings;

- maladaptive emotional responses which may be triggered and maintained by thought patterns and thinking styles.

A particularly helpful volume which demonstrates the effectiveness of this approach is Jones and Ramchandani (1999), **Child Sexual Abuse, Informing Practice from Research**. The text outlines the ways professionals can help sexually abused children and their families. It describes ways in which intervention can improve the outcome for the children and parents concerned. It includes an evidence-based approach through an extensive review of available research, together with helpful summaries of the implications for practice.

In summary

Cognitive-behavioural methods have been demonstrated to be effective in relation to a range of client groups and several areas of work. These include: offending behaviour (Hollin, 1990; Home Office, 1998; McGuire, (ed.) 1995); the management of child-behaviour (Herbert, 1981; 1987; 1989; 1995; Roner, 1993); in child abuse and neglect (Iwaniec, 1995; Jones and Ramchandani, 1999); with adult survivors of sexual abuse (Jehu, 1992) and in a broad range of other applications with children and adults (Cigno and Bourn (eds.), 1999; Scott, 1989; Sheldon, 1995).

Eco-systems theory

History

The ecological perspective is well established in the social sciences (Siporin, 1975; Maluccio, 1981; Garbarino, 1982). It has emerged as the most comprehensive unifying framework, drawing from ethology, ecological psychology and ethnology. The framework presented is based on a cluster of key ideas, as summarised from Allen-Meares and Lane (1987):

- the person-environment relationship is continuous;

- person, behaviour and environment are mutually inter-dependent;

- systems theory is useful to analyse the ecology of the person in the situation;

- behaviour is site specific;

- assessment and evaluation are through direct observation of the person-environment system;

- behaviour is the outcome of transactions between the person and the environment;

- behavioural science should seek to understand and analyse these interactions.

Current practice

The ecological approach takes a holistic view of the person in their environment and has the capacity for incorporating other approaches. Assessment will therefore gather data giving equal emphasis to the person, their environment and the interaction. The fact that data is collected in relation to all variables makes the approach holistic. The refocusing debate on child maltreatment has brought the ecological perspective into the foreground as the multi-dimensional aspects of poverty, neglect and maltreatment are researched and evidenced (Belsky, 1993; Cicchetti and Lynch, 1993; Widom, 1996).

In summary

The ecological approach has strength because it is open, integrative, inclusive, holistic and potentially culturally sensitive. Despite the recent debate in *Families in Society* (Wakefield, 1996 (1) and (2); Gitterman, 1996) it still has credibility as a unifying theory because:

- there has always been a tension in social work between the wider social policy context and focusing in the specific needs of an individual;

- social work assessments need to be aware of the larger picture but also have to operate specifically in the minutiae of immediate family difficulties.

Assessments can draw on an ecological mind-set as a broad base for initial assessments, while subsequent planning can be focused on specific applications of systems theory to identified areas of need. There are useful outlines of the use of systems theory in this way in the core literature (eg. Compton and Galaway, 1989, pp. 140-2). There are also examples of intervention with children and their families based on applied systems theory (eg. Reder, Duncan and Gray, 1993, p. 28) . The ecological framework seems to be the only one capable of embracing within in it the detail of other theories and methods. Stevenson (1998, pp. 16-1) helpfully shows how an ecological approach to understanding the child and their family is useful for assessing the factors which are contributing to the neglect of a particular child, so that a co-ordinated plan for intervention can be constructed. She says of the ecological approach (p. 19) 'though it is theoretical it is very practical; it provides a kind of map to guide us through very confusing terrain'.

Social work methods

The following section looks at some examples of identifiable social work methods which have drawn on these theories. Some are clearly linked to a particular theory and others draw on a combination of psychological and sociological theories. They also demonstrate how theory becomes integrated into practice through social work processes.

Crisis-intervention

History

Crisis-intervention is based on psychodynamic theory but also incorporates some cognitive understandings (Coulshed, 1991). It arose from attempts to provide a focused, brief form of therapy. The 'brief therapy' concept was one which matched social workers' aspirations to focus their own work more precisely. It was adopted into social work literature in the 1960s and 1970s (Caplan, 1964; Pittman, 1966; Golan, 1981).

Current practice

People who seek social work attention are often in a state of distress. Whether this can be defined as a crisis is debatable, according to O'Hagan (1992). Others such as Caplan (1964) would describe a 'crisis' as a temporary period of upset and disequilibrium, sometimes provoked by a transition or a traumatic event, where the person's usual abilities to manage are temporarily immobilised. It is, therefore, the person's perception of events which defines the state of crisis. 'One person's 'crisis' is another person's ecstasy', (O'Hagan, 1992 p. 139). Writers such as Golan (1981) and Roberts and Nee (1980) describe a crisis as having identifiable phases, which are:

- the precipitating event and perception;

- the upset;

- inability to use previously tried coping methods and disequilibrium;

- the potential for hope;

- the intervention which links current difficulties to past coping strategies;

- resolution or homeostasis restored within a few weeks (4-6).

In summary

The strength of crisis intervention in relation to assessment is that it helps the practitioner to understand why people react to similar stresses in different ways. It relates acute presenting problems to the notion of short-term intervention. In addition, it enables individuals to consider the ways they adapt to a crisis so that they may be able to react more autonomously in future in a similar situation. An assessment based on this approach results in minimal intervention which aims to build on strengths and restore service users to their usual functioning within a brief and specified time. It supports coping responses and is not deterministic.

Task-centred practice

History

Task-centred social work is a framework for practice, developed within social work, based on ego-psychology and the use of a contract. It is a focused way of supporting the service user to resolve identified key areas in their lives which are difficult. The origins of the method can be found in American literature in the 1960s and 1970s (Reid and Shyne, 1969; Reid and Epstein, 1972; 1976).

Current practice

Task-centred work and the use of contracts quickly became established in an attempt to avoid long-term interventions which encouraged dependency with its subsequent resource implications and to avoid inappropriate over-involvement. The most influential proponents of the approach were Reid and Shyne (1969) who suggested that brief work could produce as good results as long-term intervention. The task-centred approach can be seen as applicable to a problem solving framework requiring:

- service user agreement;

- an open agenda about service user and worker activities;

- specificity about concrete goals and tasks;

- allocation of tasks;

- time limits;

- review and evaluation;

- reciprocal accountability (both worker and service user taking responsibility for outcomes).

This approach emphasises the importance that the tasks selected are achievable and structured.

In summary

There is nothing inherently new in task-centred practice, but it is an approach which emphasises a service user's personal resources and strengths. Assessment focuses on the here and now and social workers have consistently found this approach to practice useful and applicable (Doel and Marsh, 1992). It is in itself a systematic model moving from assessment, through intervention to review. It embodies a partnership approach.

Family therapy

History

Family therapy draws on psychodynamic, social learning and eco-systems theory to offer a range of approaches to working with families. The genre has been developed over the last forty years in child psychiatry and child and family guidance settings. It is difficult to describe it as one unified approach since family therapists work diversely from a varied literature. However, it is succinctly defined by Gorell Barnes (1994, p. 946) as follows:

> The term family therapy encompasses three things: an observational philosophy, an approach to treating problems in families and a number of methods of treatment. It considers problems in the context both of intimate relationships and of the wider social network of which the family is a part. The aim of treatment is to bring about a change in interactions between dysfunctionally connected parts of a social system.

Current practice

The defining feature of family therapy is that the therapist targets the family system, rather than the individual, for intervention. This is a specific application of a systems approach. The family is worked with as a group by the therapist who assesses the functioning of the family and intervenes in relation to family interactions and styles. By changing the family system, the roles of the individuals can be changed towards more satisfying ways of relating.

Gorrell Barnes (1994) gives a definitive account, describing the empirical base, history and methodology of different approaches (eg. systemic; structural; strategic; conjoint), as well as ways in which practitioners have taken account of socio-economic, cultural and structural variables in families. She concludes (1994, p. 959) that:

> Research tentatively suggests that intervention focused at both levels (family and child) will have a more enduring effect than focusing on the problem alone.

There is a substantial literature which can inform social workers about the diversity of family therapy approaches (Erickson and Hogan, 1972; Minuchin, 1974; Walrond-Skinner, 1976; Hoffman, 1981; Lau, 1984; Will and Wrate, 1985; Gorrell Barnes, 1994). By far the most extensive, informative and detailed, however, are the two volumes by Bentovim, Gorrell Barnes and Cooklin (1982). A special issue of the Family Therapy Journal (1995, Vol 21(4)) sets out in a series of articles both the practice and research status of the genre as it then stood. There is some accessible and applicable literature (Paquin and Bushorn, 1991). Current applications would be found in:

- child guidance settings;

- some hospital social work departments;

- family work in the community;

- family conferences and meetings;

- family work in voluntary sector settings (eg Family Service Units) and some family centres;

- conciliation services;

- family court welfare teams.

In summary

Family therapy has generated a substantial clinical research literature in relation to family functioning. Its dissemination has been useful in helping practitioners to comprehend family dynamics and to work with an understanding of family systems. The strengths of the method are that treating the family as a unit for intervention may be more effective and far reaching than treating the individual alone. Information is gained directly by observing and listening to all family members together who can also be enabled to work out solutions together. Its disadvantage is the advanced level of knowledge and skill which is needed to practice effectively.

3 'The Child, the Family and the Outside World'

Introduction

This chapter considers some of the child development research findings and literature which are available to inform social workers who are assessing children and families in their communities and homes. For the purposes of this review the organisational structure used by D. W. G. Winnicott in his seminal work *The Child, the Family and the Outside World* (1964) is followed. Winnicott expressed his understanding of the child in the context of society when addressing an inter-disciplinary group of professionals (1966, pp. 209, 240) as follows:

> Remember the individual child, and the child's developmental process, and the child's distress, and the child's need for personal help and the child's ability to use personal help, while of course remembering the importance of the family and the various school groups and all the other groups that lead on to the one we call society.
>
> and
>
> The family leads on to all manner of groupings that get wider and wider until they reach the size of local society and society in general.

The value of a developmental mind-set to assessment is relevant at all levels of intervention. As Jones (1997, p. 522) asserts in relation to the maltreated child:

> The developmental approach allows us to develop a model that illustrates the multi-faceted nature of the key influences upon a child's development.

The child

Whatever position the assessor takes in relation to psychological theory, this only deals with explanations of behaviour. We also need to know whether a child's behaviour is appropriate to his or her age and circumstances. This calls for a sound knowledge of child development along the key dimensions of cognitive, social and emotional development, and the interaction between children and significant others (attachment). Social work assessment is normally concerned with identifying when children's developmental needs are not being met. This is reflected in the definition of a child in need in the Children Act 1989.

Under the Act (s17.(10)) a child is defined as being in need if:

> (a)   he is unlikely to achieve or maintain, or have the opportunity of achieving or maintaining, a reasonable standard of health or development without the provision for him of services by a local authority under this part;
>
> (b)   his health or development is likely to be significantly impaired, or further impaired, without the provision for him of such services; or
>
> (c)   he is disabled.
>
> Development means physical, intellectual, emotional, social or behavioural development, and health means physical or mental health.

This includes children who may not yet be suffering significant harm, but who are likely to unless something is done.

There are some classic texts which help us understand the needs of children. For example, Maslow (1943) constructed a hierarchy of needs as follows:

● physiological (food, warmth, shelter);

● security (protection from danger and deprivation);

● social (companionship, communal activities);

● egotistical (self-esteem, sense of achievement);

● psychological (growth, development).

Seminal is Kelmer Pringle's (1980, p. 34) four-fold categorisation:

● love and security;

- new experiences;

- praise and recognition;

- responsibility.

These needs are described as central to humans across the life-span. Black (1990) develops these further and categorises needs as:

- physical care;

- affection;

- security;

- stimulation;

- innate potential;

- guidance and control;

- responsibility; independence.

She quotes Cooper (1985) for a list of deficits, which are:

- death, damage, deprivation;

- disturbance in development;

- delay in language and speech development;

- distorted perceptions;

- demanding behaviour; delinquency;

- detachment.

The literature's importance for practitioners undertaking assessments is that it gives them essential knowledge about children's needs across a range of dimensions:

- physical and developmental needs;

- cognitive and learning needs;

- social (environmental) needs;

- emotional and affectional needs;

- behavioural presentation.

Another useful formulation is that of Jones (1997, p. 536) who lists parental responsibilities for meeting childrens' needs as:

- provision of adequate food and shelter;

- obtainment of necessary medical care;

- protection from harm (abuse and neglect);

- security of affective relationships;

- responsiveness to the child's emotional needs;

- discipline and guidance of behaviour;

- inculcation of moral values;

- provision of new experiences;

- assisting a child in problem solving.

The developmental approach has many advantages because of the wealth of established and current research about what appears to be universal to children; how to explain individual differences; how to understand the relationship of behaviour to context; the influence of neighbourhood, cultural background, social and economic situations. This can help practitioners to balance genetic and environmental factors in their thinking. A holistic assessment will consider the interactions between biological and environmental determinants.

It is important that social workers have a grounding in what is normal child development in order to make informed assessments. Social workers will find the following reviews of research findings useful. For example, 'broad-based life-span books' collate the outcomes of research in terms of physical, cognitive, behavioural, affective and social development. Bee (1995, sixth edition) integrates into an accessible format findings from medicine, sociology, psychology, demography, business and economics, taking a topic based approach to child development. This is an excellent first reference point for practitioners.

A similar reference text is Mussen et al. (1990, seventh edition). This is organised differently, in that it takes an 'age phases approach' (pre-birth; infants and toddlers; early and middle childhood; adolescence). This is a useful reader because it reviews physical, biological, cognitive and social development and looks at the influence of family, peers and media as contexts. The broad-based literature is a starting point for identifying children 'in need' whose development is likely to be impaired.

A key issue is knowing what is normal at each stage of development. There are many detailed books on what is age appropriate development in childhood. Sylva and Lunt (1995) and Lindon (1996) are introductory texts which offer an accurate overview of child development. Sheridan's (1997) more comprehensive work on the early years, now revised and updated, includes the original detailed schedules on child development with some additional material on special needs. This is a key text on early years development. Particularly helpful for assessment is the checklist of support services for children with special needs.

Another resource is Holt (1991), a text aimed at giving paediatricians a comprehensive outline of child development from conception to adolescence. This draws on findings from medicine, psychology, education and therapy, illustrated with charts and pictorial representations of children at various developmental stages, which are very helpful, particularly for the inexperienced or beginning practitioner.

The literature on play and childhood is vast and it is impossible to comprehend the needs of children without some reference to material about what might be usual. Books such as Einion (1985), Bruner et al. (1985) and Fraiberg (1995) are helpful. Also relevant is the important work by Rutter et al. (1994, third edition), a definitive set of edited research papers in respect of the multi-dimensional aspects of child psychiatry.

Rutter remains a pivotal writer both in terms of appraising past research and pointing to future developments. *Maternal Deprivation Re-assessed* (1981) is significant in rescuing the work of Bowlby from misunderstanding; promoting findings of multiple attachments in children, including fathers (1981, p. 127); highlighting the possible loss associated with poor experiences of care (not just mother absence); shedding light on individual differences to loss related to secure attachment; establishing the concept of resilience; as well as identifying areas for future research.

The emphasis in the literature seems to have been on early childhood. As Skuse and Bentovim (1994) comment, 'despite the ubiquitous emphasis on the dependent pre-school child, in the literature on physical and emotional maltreatment, let us not forget the vulnerable adolescent'. For assessing the needs of adolescents, five texts are particularly useful:

- Rutter (1995) has edited an overarching compilation of findings from research relevant to the difficulties experienced by teenagers. The volume addresses factors which create risk; factors which seem protective; interventions which promote better coping with the challenges young people face and which seem to reduce disorder.

- Cleaver (Department of Health, 1996) provides an overview of three research studies on adolescents, identifying issues and resources needed by young people.

- Sinclair et al. (1995) analyse assessment processes in some local authorities with adolescents. The findings point to a lack of clarity in process and concepts in assessment which have consequences for service provision.

- Herbert (1987) offers a practical book for parents and practitioners on understanding and managing adolescent behaviour.

- Neville et al. (1998) address the problems and challenges of living with teenagers from a social learning theory perspective.

There are critical periods in children's development of which social workers need to be aware. For example, the early years are critical for physical and speech development. Murray's work (1997, p. 253) gives 'some support to the idea that there is a sensitive early developmental period in respect of cognitive development, although there is little known of the precise parameters involved'. Conversely, trauma and stressful experiences are being considered as possibly permanently changing responses in maltreated individuals (Perry, 1993) and difficult to remedy subsequently. This implies that effective intervention to compensate for deficits at the appropriate time is critical. These American studies into neurological deficits caused by maltreatment provide evidence that an approach to children's services which supports the optimum nurture and wellbeing of children within an ecological, multi-dimensional framework is the most likely to produce good outcomes for children (Belsky, 1993; Puttnam, 1998). Guralnick (1997) also evidences the importance of effective early intervention.

In assessing children there are various tools used by other professionals, for example, health visitors, educational psychologists, teachers and doctors. However, until recently, very little has been specifically designed for use by social workers. Since 1995 the Department of Health's *Looking after Children* records have been influential. They are based on seven developmental dimensions and thoroughly validated in a community based study. These take account of age, gender and identity. They are designed to ensure that practitioners focus on the key issues in the healthy development of children:

- health;

- education;

- identity;

- family and social relationships;

- social presentation;

- emotional and behavioural development;

- self-care skills.

The materials pose a series of age-related questions that seek to ascertain whether children looked after are receiving the type of care that a reasonable parent might be expected to provide within each of the dimensions. The Department of Health et al's Assessment Framework (2000), includes further materials specifically developed for use by social workers (Department of Health and Cleaver, 2000). These can be found in the chapter which considers resources.

In addition to age, gender, identity and the other dimensions defined by the *Looking After Children* records, there are other key issues which are also important for consideration in the assessment process. In particular, social workers need to be aware of issues of attachment and resilience.

Attachment

Attachment issues are addressed by Howe (1995) who expressly links attachment theory to social work practice and the assessment process (1995, p. 189). Fahlberg's schedules (1981; 1982) are useful frameworks for thinking about the stages of child placement and the relevance of aspects of child development to social work planning. Attachment in relation to the life span is explored by Parkes et al. (1991) in a volume which disseminates some more recent theoretical contributions, many of which are as important in assessing parents' capacity and specific aspects of children's experience. Studies on attachment have developed from a child and carer focus to attempting to consider the complexities of the multiple attachments a child may have.

Young Children's Relationships (Dunn, 1993) examines the contexts of attachments through childhood. Dunn is already established for her work on siblings (1984). This volume is part of a series by Sage which seeks to explore children in their contexts and shed light on individual differences. Other authors who contribute to our understanding of children's relationships are Lamb (1997) on the role of the father in child development, and Erwin (1993) on peer relations. Both these volumes consider a range of factors in their specific domains. Motherhood has also received critical attention (Schaffer, 1977; Phoenix et al., 1991).

Resilience

Resilience, and the linked concept of buffers against adversity, is an important focus of research attention. Rutter (1985) identifies the importance of protective factors and interactive processes which suggest the need not only for a multi-dimensional model of assessment but also for suitable intervention at critical periods. More recently Gilligan (1997) has been discussing resilience in children and how it might be assessed. He writes primarily in relation to placement planning but provides some broad measures for assessing the outcomes of resilience in children and young people. Understanding the concepts of buffers against adversity and resilience is essential for assessing need and the impact of intervention in a child's life at an early stage (Widom, 1996). Cicchetti et al. (1993) demonstrate that maltreated children, when compared with a group of peers, appear less resilient across a range of functions. Such work points to the consequences of maltreatment as long-term and argues for early preventive action.

The complexity of assessing child development is the consistent feature in the literature reviewed (Rutter et al. 1994; Widom, 1996; Gilligan, 1997). As Cicchetti and Rizley (1981, p. 34) write 'the empirical study of child development is a perplexing scientific problem for which we have no ready answers or simple solutions'. While this complexity has to be acknowledged, some of the well evidenced trends such as the long-term outcomes of early deprivation or the importance of understanding a child's attachments are firm planks to rely upon in thinking about children's services.

Disabled children

The complexity issues are particularly highlighted in relation to the assessment of disabled children. These children are clearly designated as children in need by the Children Act 1989. Local authorities have a duty to provide services to promote their health and development. It is argued that practitioners should seek to offer appropriate services through inclusion rather than exclusion (Hardiker, Seden and Barker, 1995). Assessment should be combined wherever possible with education and health, so as to avoid multiple assessments and to achieve a comprehensive evaluation. Liaison with housing and benefits agencies is also important. However, findings from the Joseph Rowntree Foundation (1998) show that problems of professionals not being able to communicate easily with disabled children lead to inadequate assessments.

Research suggests that the families of disabled children are particularly vulnerable to stress, especially those in socio-economically disadvantaged circumstances. Beresford (1995) explored the needs and circumstances of over a thousand parents caring for a severely disabled child. The findings confirm that some families were particularly vulnerable to high levels of unmet need. These were lone parents, minority ethnic group families and parents of the most severely disabled children.

The socio-economic framework for disabled children together with a framework for analysis are outlined by Hardiker et al. (1995) who describe service principles and good practice in family support. Friel (1995) outlines the fundamental principles of the Education Code of Practice: identification of the need for assessment as early as possible; by the appropriate agency; resulting in a clear report; which both takes a multi-disciplinary approach and also ascertains the wishes and feelings of the child (1995, p. 38). This practical guide for parents and professionals details law, assessment and practice, addressing fully the potential for children being 'caught between the acts'.

Farrell (1995) considers special needs from an educational perspective. Russell (1997) writes usefully on strategies for supporting families. Dale (1996) has produced a comprehensive reader and resource book which describes a practice framework for thinking about partnership with children and their families. BAAF's (1982) *From Asthma to Thalassaemia* provides basic information on a range of children's illnesses and their treatment, often inadequately understood by social work practitioners. A report for the National Autistic Society (Brady, 1997) surveys the services and effectiveness for families with an autistic family member. She argues both for a family support worker and an integrated approach between health, education and social services.

Sloper (1997) identifies a range of dimensions for assessment; parental tasks; parental distress; coping strategies; urgent needs; role of services. This is detailed and practical, containing substantial quotations from parents. For example, she quotes one parent as saying:

> I think that if professionals listened more to the parent, then a lot of situations would not crop up. I remember when I did not know where to turn and there seemed to be a brick wall between me and the professionals.

Westcott (1992) has been seminal in disseminating knowledge about abuse among disabled children and in developing a review of the literature and communication tools. Howlin and Jones (1996) consider the complexities and possible practitioner bias in the use of facilitated communication methods. They conclude that the methods are helpful, but worker awareness of the dimensions of holistic assessment reduces bias. Facilitation of communication runs the risk that the facilitator's preconceptions control outcomes.

The family

Winnicott (1960) famously wrote that 'there is no such thing as an infant', meaning that children should be viewed in relationship with their principal carer(s). He also took the view that paediatricians should intervene as little as possible as 'mothers and babies generally know best' and that mothers only need be 'good enough', rather than perfect.

Whether a child is cared for by a mother, father or other carers, the principle remains that the relationship between the parties is crucial. Children shape carers as much as they are moulded by their carers (Rutter, 1981).

Much of the thinking that has informed practitioners over the years is enshrined in documentation which assesses people on their capacity to look after other people's children. Guidance on this is published by the National Foster Care Association in a series of useful papers, including one on the assessment of foster carers. NFCA's mission is to 'ensure that all children and young people who are fostered receive the highest standards of care'. The publications are designed to help those concerned with this work. Adcock and White's (1985) work on parenting has also been widely used.

Parents have a responsibility to meet a child's needs as spelt out in the Children Act 1989. It is also recognised that parents have their own needs and that in meeting them they may enhance their ability to carry out their parental responsibility more autonomously. Assessing parents for the provision of support under s17 should be carried out in a non-stigmatising manner. It is important when assessing parents' ability to care for their children to identify strengths and protective factors as well as highlighting areas where there are difficulties and support may be needed.

There are circumstances where children are at risk of suffering significant harm and the courts are involved. Reder and Lucey (1995) provide a synthesis of literature which is primarily designed for use by practitioners compiling assessments for family court proceedings. Nevertheless it is useful information for all those responsible for undertaking assessments of children and parents. Their assessment framework is helpful, but more valuable is the brief guidance on how to weigh up and use the information obtained in decision making, which factors to look for and their possible significance.

One of the problems in assessing parenting capacity has been a tendency to make assumptions that parents who are capable in some areas of their lives are adequately meeting all the needs of their children. For example, the inquiry into the death of Jasmine Beckford, *A Child in Trust* (1985), revealed that social workers assumed that because the father was in work and the home was well cared for, the child was also well cared for. Campion (1995) presents an analysis identifying the key issues on which practitioners need to focus in assessing parenting. These include:

● physical care;

● health care;

● protection from danger;

● education;

● adequate nutrition;

● opportunities for development;

● preparation for adulthood and independence;

● development of self-esteem;

● opportunity for spirituality, identity, affection and trust;

● social and cognitive skills;

- stability of close relationships;

- economic support;

- moral guidance;

- model adult behaviour, and self regulation.

Family therapy practitioners have developed models for assessing family dynamics and systems (Miller et al., 1994; Hamilton and Orme, 1990; Gaudin et al., 1996). These studies are largely concerned with the dimensions of functioning in neglectful families or families in treatment following identified deficits in parenting. In North American clinical writing much seems to be claimed for family functioning scales and there appears to be a spate of activity to evaluate and validate the findings. Care needs to be taken to ensure that if practitioners are using these time-consuming methods they also have the training and resources to use them effectively. The indicators (or functioning categories), however, seem well tested and can establish dimensions for complex assessment. Gaudin et al. (1996) produce a detailed assessment and intervention schedule based on specific indicators, specific kinds of families and specified, linked, intervention methods. The particular methods identified include parent education, support and other methods familiar to social workers. Gaudin et al. (1996) usefully identify differences between neglectful families and argue for the necessity of differential individual family assessments across the key dimensions of:

- problem solving abilities;

- communication patterns;

- roles;

- affective communication;

- affective involvement;

- behaviour control.

Another area which has relevance for assessment is the literature about parent training (Scott, 1983; Edwards, 1995; Neville et al., 1996; 1998). Scott and Neville report positive outcomes from these methods. However, Edwards (p. 257) sounds a note of caution about who benefits from such programmes. She writes, 'in perceiving parenting skills as a body of knowledge which can be taught, they *(the professionals)* provide and render visible a strategy for improving the lives of women and children with whom they work' *in lieu of offering resources.*

As good attachment is extremely important for children's development so bonding from parent to child (parental empathy) emerges as a crucial dimension of parenting. Much attention has been given to empathy in adult human relationships (Rogers, 1961; Egan, 1990) but little attention to measures of empathy between adults and children. Rosenstein (1995) suggests that a measure of parental empathy should be part of the risk assessment tools used by child protection practitioners. Specifically she suggests (1995, p. 1358) that the following questions be added to parent/caretaker assessments and scored moderate, serious or severe:

- Is the parent able to individualise the child?

- Is the parent able to describe the child in terms of the child's needs?

- Does the parent expect the child to satisfy parental needs?

Rosenstein (1995) links high levels of parental empathy with better outcomes for children. This is consistent with a view of Cameron (1997). He shares some preliminary findings from the child development work currently being undertaken by Murray at Reading University. Parental empathy is a key factor in positive child self-identity. A parent who can demonstrate accurate empathy (not to be confused with sympathy) is more likely to understand and respond appropriately to a child's needs.

A further point emphasised in the principles accompanying the Children Act 1989 is that there is room for considerable diversity in family styles. Societal expectations of parents change over time. Recent papers have helped to disaggregate the factors discrete to parenting from those concerned with the life styles of those who happen to be parents. For example, Flaks et al. (1995) undertook a comparative study of lesbian and heterosexual parents and their children. They evaluated the children's cognitive functioning and behavioural adjustment, and the parents' relationship. The survey reveals no significant differences in the children or parenting, except that the lesbian couples show more parenting awareness. This kind of study is helpful in establishing a knowledge base for assessment where ideology rather than reasoned judgement might prevail.

The strengths approach (Saleebey, 1997) to assessing parents and families appears most likely to produce co-operative outcomes. Assessment frameworks for working with parents should facilitate carers to perceive and meet the needs of their children themselves. Neighbourhood approaches emphasise supporting families before difficulties arise which may then require complex interventions. Frost (1997, p. 210) describes and evaluates one such approach, a befriending, family support service. Furthermore, he suggests the outcome is 'value for money'. He writes:

> Given the success rate of seventy-nine per cent, we can estimate that of the 230 interventions at least the possibility of 180 people being looked after has been diverted. Using these indicators, we can say that this makes this particular example of family support remarkable 'value for money' and suggests that similar possibilities exist in other fields of family support.

Balancing state intervention with family autonomy is a delicate matter. Hardiker, Exton and Barker (1996, p. 3) express concern about 'the inequalities, inconsistencies and exclusions in children's lives and the extent to which these are embedded in current public policy. We are also concerned about achieving a balance of responsibility between families and society'. Mooney and Munton (1997, p. 30) argue that, 'given family patterns where parental employment is usual, good quality early childhood services have a key role to play in the holistic development of children's cognitive, language, social and emotional development'.

The effectiveness of early contextual intervention is assessed by Guralnick (1997, p. 5) who summarises relevant first generation research and outlines areas for further investigation. He offers a synthesis of family action modes which need to be assessed. They are:

● the quality of the parent child interaction;

- the extent to which the family provides the child with diverse and appropriate experiences with the surrounding social and physical environment;

- the way in which the family ensures the child's health and safety.

He concludes that 'taken together, it is the complex interplay of these three influential factors that constitutes the foundation of contemporary developmental models'. Thus, the family is important in ensuring the child's well-being is paramount, but it is assisted or made more difficult by its context and external social environment available.

Recent work on parental capacity (Cleaver et al. 1999) suggests that there are many factors which inhibit a parent's ability to respond to their child's needs. Assessment recording forms have been developed (Department of Health and Cleaver, 2000) which are designed to assess parental capacity to respond to children's developmental needs within their wider family and environmental context. This work will provide useful, detailed records which social workers can use for analysis and planning, and which managers can use for aggregating information for planning purposes. The parental capacity factors identified as fundamental to the Assessment Framework (Department of Health et al, 2000) are:

- basic care;

- ensuring safety;

- emotional warmth;

- stimulation;

- guidance and boundaries;

- stability.

The records recognise that no family can bring up children without the support of services, such as health and education, and reliable informal social networks and community resources. The conditions which promote successful parenting have been summarised (Aldgate and Colman, 1999, p. 10) as:

- sufficient financial and material support to meet children's basic needs for food, warmth and shelter;

- an ability to protect children from danger;

- an understanding of children's needs at different ages and stages of development and taking pleasure from children's progress;

- the oppportunity to be valued as an adult;

- an ability to access primary health care for self and children;

- an ability to support children's educational progress.

A constellation of factors contribute to achieving optimal outcomes for the developing child. These include: the needs of the individual child; the ability of parents and carers to respond adequately to those needs; the contribution of the wider community; support services such as health and education provided by the state.

The outside world

The third key area to be considered in the assessment of children is the relationship between the family and the neighbourhood in which they live. The biggest shift in child development theory has been away from assessing the mother-child dyad to looking at children in the context of their wider family and the contribution made by communities to their upbringing (Jack, 1996). There is a consequent awareness that simple cause and effect analysis of events in children's lives is limiting. It is suggested by de Winter (1997, p. 150) that growing up is a dynamic process. It is influenced by factors in the 'immediate vicinity', the school and neighbourhood. Improving matters within family relationships alone is not enough and a more holistic approach is needed. For example, 'by systematically checking the various environmental aspects, professional people can form an opinion on the situation in which young people grow up' (de Winter, 1997).

It is important to consider the relationship between children, their caretakers and society whilst acknowledging the balance of responsibilities between them (Moss and Petrie, 1996). The welfare of children cannot be separated from that of their families and neighbours. The strengthening of families and neighbourhoods then becomes the first place to address maltreatment and disadvantage (significant harm). As Nelson (1997) writes: 'The welfare of children is inseparable from the capacity of families... the capacity of families is inseparable from the health and vitality of the communities that surround them'.

Poverty and its associated factors can act cumulatively to impede successful parenting and increase children's vulnerability. The clusters of indicators which may contribute to this can be identified from mild and moderate concerns before they become risk factors. Bebbington and Miles (1989) identified the prevalence of six such factors identifiable with families whose children come into care:

- household on income support;

- children living in a single adult household;

- four or more children in the household;

- children of mixed ethnic origin;

- family living in a privately rented home;

- family with one person or more per room.

Poverty and environmental disadvantage remain a major cause of vulnerability in childhood.

Therefore, assessment will need to understand and weigh the individual and structural dimensions of children's ecologies and consider where to target any needed compensation, rather than focus too narrowly on the child and family alone. The developmental approach to understanding children, their families and environments is underpinned and supported by a substantial raft of empirically based literature (Bentovim, 1997; Cichetti and Lynch, 1993; Belsky, 1993). The literature also evidences the difficulties of costly remedial action. Supporting families to achieve good outcomes for their own children in their own neighbourhoods is a well evidenced strategy.

4 *Working in a Multi-Cultural Context*

Introduction

Some basic needs and parental responses might be said to be universal, but care has to be taken to avoid stereotyping and value judgements. There are different styles of parenting, and family patterns vary according to culture and community. The Children Act 1989 requires local authorities to have due regard to the religion, race, culture and language of the child in relation to foster placements, other accommodation and other interventions. Assessing children's needs according to dimensions based on child development enables social workers to consider these issues for each child, for example, as they relate to identity. Recent work by Dutt and Phillips (1999) relates the use of the *Looking After Children* records to assessment of the needs of black children. This chapter explores some of the literature about assessment as it relates to multi-cultural contexts and religious persuasion, bearing in mind that recognising racial and cultural diversity adds richness to understanding what factors will promote a child's welfare.

Stereotypical assumptions

A criticism of assessment has been that the methods and underpinning knowledge have been inadequate for practice. Good outcomes for children have been blocked by stereotypical assumptions. Ahmed et al. (1986, p. 3) underline three important areas in relation to the provision of welfare services for black children and their families:

- the importance of focusing on strengths;

- having an understanding of the politics of race and its impact on families and services;

- working for change which combats the impact of racism on individuals and families.

Changes in ethnic diversity in populations need to be acknowledged (Coombe and Little, 1986) but not in ways which confuse family support practices with cultural relativism in child maltreatment (Seden, 1995). Cultural sensitivity includes an appreciation of the significance of moral and spiritual dimensions in the lives of children and families as well as race, culture and language in order to appreciate the needs of the 'whole child' (Bradford, 1995; Seden, 1995; Crompton, 1996).

It is particularly important to consider the needs of dual heritage children and young people. First, because they are are over-represented in care (Bebbington and Miles, 1989). Second, because there is a risk of having no affiliation to either 'black' or 'white' social groupings. Tizard and Phoenix's study (1993) of the young people's own views of their identity is helpful for policy and practice. The respondents valued their self-defined identities, which were shaped by home, neighbourhood, media and school. They also valued clear anti-racist policies with strategies for implementation in their schools.

Black minority ethnic groups remain apparently under-represented as service users receiving preventive and supportive social services provision, but over-represented in those aspects of social services activity which involve social control (Lago and Thompson, 1996; Tunstill and Aldgate, 1999). Research still grapples with the ambiguities of findings which indicate that black children and their families receive fewer services than their caucasian counterparts, as it remains difficult to disaggregate the effects of variables such as culture, racism, and socio-economic groupings (Courtney et al., 1996; Widom, 1996).

Family diversity

The diversity of 21st Century family groupings means that practitioners need to be aware of the family's culture. As Pinderhughes (1995, p. 131) writes:

> The rapid increase around the world of inter-actions among people of diverse cultural and social backgrounds along with (1) major shifts in how the family is defined, and (2) increasing fragmentation and disconnection among families, will place extraordinary demands on family practitioners in the 21st century.

To help families from a variety of backgrounds, social workers will need to address cultural factors if they are to be 'flexible, open thinkers who are comfortable with diversity' (Pinderhughes, 1995, p. 139). Empowerment literature would suggest that assessing families, using a combined family strengths and eco-systems approach, is most likely to ensure the practitioners will take account of race, religion, language and culture (Laird, 1995; Pinderhughes, 1995).

Sensitive practice

Pedersen (1997), writing for assessors in a counselling context, contributes some helpful pointers as to how social workers might think about assessment. He writes that, as all assessments have a cross cultural dimension, there must always be a focus on accurate cultural understanding. In summary, he suggests that to achieve this, practitioners need to avoid:

- defining reality according to one set of cultural assumptions and stereotypes;

- insensitivity to cultural variations among individuals;

- assuming their own view is the only legitimate one;

- protecting their own unreasoned assumptions without evidence;

- encapsulating assumptions in a technique based job-orientation;

- failing to accommodate other people's view points.

A more comprehensive understanding of alternatives in personal beliefs and family values is wanted, including religious beliefs. Further, practitioners will need to:

- affirm and recognise richness in diverse family structures;

- affirm the capacity of all families to find solutions;

- recognise that traditional methods have not always met the needs of ethnic minorities and other cultural groups;

- recognise and value diversity in populations;

- consider how an individual may view the helping relationship;

- consider how the service user in their own culture usually solves problems;

- endeavour to be informed about the background of others;

- communicate in a manner sensitive to other cultural values;

- feel comfortable to ask questions about customs or values with which they are not familiar.

In conclusion, it can be said that assessment frameworks alone cannot facilitate an outcome which is culturally appropriate but that work has been done to assist practitioners take account of issues which are significant to the development of black children and significant to a family's religious persuasion. Social workers undertaking assessments with children and their families need to have knowledge and awareness of the diversity and flexibility of family structures in order to be open-minded, flexible and accurate in forming judgements, making plans and offering services. This sensitive awareness and ability to respond suitably to diversity of need will be very important to ensure that all families and children receive suitable support services when needed. Cultural sensitivity without the necessary action is not enough on its own. As Dungee-Anderson and Beckett (1995, p. 466) write:

> Practitioners who are self aware and knowledgeable about multi-cultural issues are able to understand and assess service users from varied backgrounds as well as offer interventions and policies which are ethnically and culturally sensitive.

And also, as the Department of Health (1998, p. 13) states:

> A balanced assessment must incorporate a cultural perspective, but guard against being over-sensitive to cultural issues at the expense of promoting the safety and well-being of the child.

5 The Inter-Agency Context of Assessment

Introduction

The assessment of children necessarily involves different dimensions and calls for inputs from different departments with different responsibilities within the Local Authority and Health Authority. For example, social services, health, education and youth services all have their part to play. The rationale for this is expressed clearly in Aldgate and Colman (1999, p. 31) as follows:

> Because children's development is multi-faceted, for the first time the Children Act introduced the idea of a range of co-ordinated local authority services being used to promote children's health and development, not just those provided by social services departments. Guidance and regulations emphasise the need for co-operation: sections 17(5), 27, and 30 provide duties and powers in relation to co-operation between and consultation with different authorities including social services, education departments and housing authorities, health authorities and independent organisations. The introduction of Children's Services Plans was designed to enable local authorities to engage in corporate planning of services for children and their families.

This chapter considers some of the findings in relation to multi-disciplinary perspectives in assessment, inter-agency communication, collaboration and joint actions in planning, which are represented in the research and literature.

Co-operation in practice

The way in which professionals work collaboratively throughout their assessment and planning for children is crucial. Success in this is important because the literature shows that failure to achieve a holistic assessment and plan will undermine opportunities for positive outcomes in children's lives (Parker et al., 1991; Ward, 1995; Birchall and Hallett, 1995; Sinclair (ed), 1995). Hallett and Birchall (1995) and Birchall and Hallett (1995) found that co-operation between agencies seemed to work well at the early stages of assessment. They also found that most professionals seemed to have an understanding of each others' perspectives and roles. However, they also found that after the initial assessment phases, social services took a lead in case-management roles in child protection cases. Research by Peel and Ward (in progress) to test indicators for need with a range of professionals in North Lincolnshire appears to be confirming that there is shared understanding between a range of professionals about assessing concerns in terms of mild, moderate and more serious, when assessing children's needs using a developmental model.

In regard to the early years, literature signposts the way for coherent inter-agency planning (Pugh, 1992; David, 1994; Sinclair et al., 1997). Resource materials and research are available in respect of children in their middle years and adolescence (Rutter, 1994; Cleaver, 1996; Aldgate and Tunstill, 1998). Research into the delivery of services to disabled children consistently shows that a unified, seamless service is desirable for such children and their families (eg. Beresford, 1995; Brady, 1997; Sloper, 1997).

At later stages of assessment and planning, Reder, Duncan and Gray (1993) suggest that issues of responsibility and accountability in respect of children at risk of suffering significant harm make relationships between disciplines less co-operative. This finding is supported by Birchall and Hallett (1995) who say (in summary) that in 'child protection' cases:

● inter-disciplinary training is not in place or sufficient;

● different perspectives are taken by paediatricians and social workers;

● role confusion and uncertainty about who should act is apparent;

● political factors and resourcing issues lead to territorial disputes;

● professional training most clearly affects the way an issue in a case scenario is viewed by a worker.

It is also clear from inquiry reports (Department of Health, 1991c) that inter-agency collaborative work needs to be improved in the interests of maltreated children. It appears that the difficulties in inter-disciplinary working in child protection cases are perhaps more about territory and resourcing, or the stress of complex work, than about the assessment approach, except when social/medical models become opposed. However, agreement that inter-agency co-operation is both necessary but hard to achieve is consistently expressed. For example, Valente (1998, pp. 42-3) writes from a practitioner perspective:

> Smooth inter-agency working does not always come naturally. It can be fraught with pressure and conflict, especially in the field of child protection where difficult, contentious decisions abound. Inter-disciplinary collaboration is not a choice… there is much to be gained by investing in positive inter-agency working. The mutual support, cross-fertilisation of ideas and pooled resources which result serve to enhance the universally agreed aim of protecting vulnerable children from harm.

Murphy (1993) also offers a practical exploration of the task of working together from a social work practitioner perspective, and explores the attitudes and skills workers need do this effectively.

Future directions

Sometimes literature about multi-disciplinary working seems written from a rather polarised perspective, yet the literature reviewed in the earlier part of this paper clearly demonstrates the overlap in the theory and knowledge base of workers in different disciplines. The development of assessment models which can be used by different agencies working together will enhance joint planning. Social workers also need to be clear where and what others contribute to the assessment of children's needs and to recognise the benefits of combining theoretical understandings.

These other professionals may include: educationalists, counsellors, doctors and other health care professionals, clinical psychologists, child carers, day care providers, voluntary sector childcare workers and others who may know a child and family well. All have a special perspective to bring to assessment, although it is always important to identify the levels of knowledge of a particular child and family and to integrate this into the overall understanding. Community resources are also an essential component of the overall picture.

The best assessment tools, for all agencies, will be those which can be used together, which keep families 'open' to professional involvement and professionals open to each other. Where families close the door to professionals, children may be at risk unobserved (Reder et al., 1993, p. 71). Children are also at risk when professionals fail to communicate and work together. This integrative approach is illustrated by Sinclair et al. (1995, p.304) who while reporting on research relating to adolescents, draw attention to some important findings which can be related to assessment generally, that is that:

> Departments need to think about developing systems that are capable of being adapted for individual cases, rather than operating a series of different models of assessment depending on how a case is classified. Without this flexible unitary approach to assessment there is a danger that the current fragmentation of assessment with its reflection in complex planning arrangements will continue.

There appears to be merit in the concept of a person-based assessment record (eg. *Looking After Children*) at all levels of intervention, which can specify needed inputs, thus drawing on the expertise of all relevant professionals, carers and communities, for a particular child. The existence of a coherent planning tool in a child's life, provides something continuous in the fragmentation and discontinuities which many children experience. Social workers whose professional expertise is in collation and brokering (Abbott, 1995; Lhullier and Martin, 1994; Hasenfeld, 1993) are well placed to coordinate such records.

Holistic problems require holistic solutions. If children are viewed ecologically, as individuals in their social and cultural environments, it follows that any action undertaken in their lives should be inter-disciplinary. In addition, if children's development is viewed as multi-dimensional, it is necessary to include the contributions of all professionals to the assessment of need. The Children Act 1989, augmented by the White Paper, *Modernising Social Services* (1998), reinforces the necessity of developing a corporate strategy for children's services. The Local Authority (1998, para.6. 27) has a duty as a whole to:

- improve the health and development of looked after children;

- determine priorities for improving support for children in need, including disabled children and those with emotional and behavioural difficulties, and set out how those priorities will be given effect;

- address housing needs of families with children in need;

- summarise the outcomes intended in youth justice, behaviour support, and early years plans, and thus bring together action on behalf of the main groups of children at risk of social exclusion.

Therefore, the mandate is established for shared budgets, inter-departmental co-operation and collaboration which encourage the development of 'joined up thinking' to address the multi-faceted needs of children.

To implement such a strategy, there must be a stong lead from elected members and chief officers, as well as effective inter-agency working to plan, manage and deliver services. Social workers and other professional workers will need to work together to overcome barriers to effective joint working and consider the findings of research (eg. Aldgate and Tunstill, 1995) which show examples of effective practice and partnership in action.

Professionals may be employed in different sectors, with different responsibilities, but there are considerable overlaps in knowledge, understandings and overall aims, which can be pooled in the interests of children and their families. It follows that, inter-disciplinary research and training have a crucial role in developing attitudes and experiences of co-operation. Knowing who should be involved is only the first stage in working towards providing a seamless inter-disciplinary service. An attitude of bridge building where commonalities are established by explicit linkages of budgets and planning infrastructure, as well as, professional understandings, training and common objectives, can best mobilise resources for the child.

In relation to assessment, a unified Assessment Framework has now been developed (Department of Health et al, 2000) specifying roles, responsibilities and contributions at all stages, which is a way of co-ordinating a continuous holistic picture of a child's needs. This will enable agencies to assess the needs of children coherently. The best assessment, using the Assessment Framework, will be systematic, structured, reflective and suited to the individual child and their family circumstances. It will identify and weigh the contributions of individual disciplines, the child and the family in relation to the understandings, actions and decisions that are made. Social workers with a heritage of working from a breadth of professional knowledge bases are ideally placed to act both as commissioners and direct providers of services for children in need within this mandate for inter-agency collaboration.

6 *Learning from Community Care Assessment*

Introduction

The NHS and Community Care Act 1990 resulted in a major shift of emphasis in services for vulnerable adults. The practice guidelines set out for the first time a model consistent with social work processes, which includes the collation, collection and analysis of information. The guidance makes it clear that the emphasis is on needs-led assessment, not fitting service users to services. Guidance says that Local Authorities have a duty to 'assess peoples' needs holistically in relation to a wide range of possible service options, rather than having separate service-led assessments' (Department of Health, 1991a).

The assessment principles as specified in the practitioner's guide are to: 'negotiate the scope of assessment; choose the setting; clarify expectations; promote participation; establish a relationship of trust; assess need; determine eligibility; set priorities; agree objectives; record the assessment' (Department of Health, 1991b). Implementation has produced some tensions and contradictions, consideration of which might be helpful in thinking about implementing the *Framework for the Assessment of Children in Need and their Families*.

The debate about need

The literature about assessment under the NHS and Community Care Act 1990 is characterised by continuous debate about what is needs-led. For example, is need defined as disadvantage? Is it defined as the right to a minimum level of provision? For example: clean water; adequate nutrition; adequate protection and housing; a non hazardous work environment; appropriate health care; security in childhood; significant primary relationships; physical security; appropriate education; safer birth control and child bearing (Doyal and Gough, 1991). Alternatively, need has been understood to encompass all the dimensions in Bradshaw's (1972) taxonomy: normative needs; felt needs; expressed needs; comparative needs. The literature is preoccupied with questions such as: What is need and who defines it? To what extent is the system needs-led? It is also suggested that unmet needs are seldom well collated and that the link between population needs and individual needs is not well documented (Percy Smith, 1996).

This debate about needs, wants and eligibility has continued in adult services, but can be avoided in relation to children's services because the criteria for defining their needs is clearly developmental, grounded in psychological literature and reflected in the philosophy of the Children Act 1989. This makes the issues of assessing need more straightforward, but it is important to note that the definitions of 'need' like those of 'abuse' are socially constructed and will be refined over time. The development (and continual updating) of tools, which are constructed from recent reseach findings (eg Ward, 1995; Department of Health and Cleaver, 2000), to assist practitioners with this task is therefore essential.

Empowerment philosophy

The empowerment philosophy which underpins the NHS and Community Care Act 1990 has not been fully realised in the early stages of implementation. Browne (1996) specifies as shortfalls: the extent to which people are informed and included in the assessment process; deficits in recording agreements in writing; administrative arrangements being difficult for users to comprehend.

Deakin (1996) agrees that the empowerment focus has been undermined by: under-resourcing (with delays undercutting principles of user choice); problems of definition and procedural obstacles (Whose needs are to be met – user or carer? What if these conflict?); service user choice (how can a user have choice when contracts are awarded in a quasi market controlled by managers?). Deakin concludes that 'the user is not at the centre of the picture in community care practice'.

However, child centred practice is already an established concept in children's services. In relation to children, empowerment relies upon adults in society fulfilling their responsibilities so that children are enabled to achieve their potential and exercise reasonable choice. The children's rights movement is providing a literature which addresses the ways and means of empowering children (Flekkoy, 1991; Knutsson, 1997). While it is likely some of the questions considered in the assessment of adults will be relevant to childrens' services a key difference is that the child and family social worker should consider the impact on the particular child of all the relevant factors in terms of both the child's current wellbeing and also the likelihood of the achievement of future optimal developmental outcomes.

Differential approaches to assessment

In adult care, differential approaches to assessment have been taken by different stake holders. Thus, assessment may be identified by managers as an important area of practice which should lead to more effective use of limited resources. Practitioners may see assessment as a means of responding to service user need. Service users and carers may be unclear about the function of assessment. There is some confusion around the concept that assessments should match needs and resources while not being resource-led. Concern is expressed that assessment becomes a tool for rationing (Powell and Goddard, 1996).

In relation to children, the assessment must draw upon a framework of developmental dimensions. The tensions of the implementation of s.17 of the Children Act 1989 and the tendency for service commissioners to prioritise risk assessment is documented and evidenced in several research studies (Department of Health, 1995; Aldgate and Tunstill, 1996; 1998) and also in Chapter 1 of this review. In the future planning of services, the assessment of the needs of children should be undertaken in the context of research into development and what is needed to produce the optimal outcome for each child in his or her particular situation.

There are some learning points from the implementation of the NHS and Community Care Act 1990 for those concerned with assessment in children's services. Aldgate and Tunstill's study (1995) of the implementation of s.17 assessments has already found that assessments of need still seemed to be service led. However, to compare 'needs-led' assessment in community care with child care assessments is not to compare like with like, as both the service user groups and the legislation are significantly different.

Assessment in child care can be linked firmly to developmental definitions of needs, which are clearly different from the needs of vulnerable older people or those experiencing mental ill health. An approach based on supporting family strengths may have more potential to be underpinned by empowerment philosophies because of the importance of existing community infrastructures (eg. schools and clinics). Some contradictions and tensions are inevitable but child centred practice does not need to conflate needs and rights, so long as children are viewed as 'citizens rather than worthy causes' (Knutsson, 1997) and the process clearly remains child centred, incorporating children's ascertainable wishes and feelings as the law directs.

Assessment can work for the betterment of children's welfare, but requires effective participation by all the identified relevant agencies. The requirement for Childrens Services Plans, taken together with the white paper, *Modernising Social Services* (1998), *Quality Protects* (1998), the new Post Qualifying Award in Child Care Framework and Curriculum Guidance (1999) and the development of an Assessment Framework for Children in Need, Department of Health et al, (2000) provide an opportunity for creative planning which considers the needs of children and their families holistically across all the stages of assessment, intervention and action.

7 *The Way Forward*

What the literature tells us

Assessment frameworks are well documented in social work literature. Two main themes predominate, assessing risk and empowerment. The safety and security of the child and legal responsibilities always come first, but child focused approaches which build on family strengths may keep families working in partnership with service providers, which will be in the long term interests of the child.

Social work processes are underpinned by psychosocial and ecological theory, from which other practice models have been developed. Regular updating of knowledge about research findings and social trends is essential so that models remain appropriate. Drawing from different disciplines should be done explicitly and from material based on evidence. Tools for assessment should be derived from empirically based research.

There is a rich and diverse literature which contributes to the understanding of the needs of the child and family in their contexts. Practitioners need to know how to use this to inform their assessments of the meaning and relevance of specific factors in children's lives. The further integration of child development theory into practice is a fundamental part of the Department of Health et al's Assessment Framework. The *Looking after Children* dimensions (Ward, 1995) have been instrumental in providing a child development framework for assessment and are built into this Guidance. The dimensions are: health; education; identity; family and social relationships; social presentation; emotional development and behaviour; self-care skills. These *Looking After Children* records already give the opportunity for children and families to be fully involved in the assessment of need and progress. They provide the basis for accountability between parents and professionals. The following aspects can be included within the assessment of the looked after child: child's perceptions of the situation; problem/s identified by referrer or parent/s; parental capacity to meet the child's needs; considerations of parental empathy; child resilience; community networks and neighbourhood resources. This approach can be applied to assessment of all children who may be in need. The assessment of children is inevitably linked to the assessment of the capacities of their parents to provide a safe and nurturing environment (Cleaver et al., 1999).

Assessment does not take place in a cultural vacuum. Social workers need to understand cultural dimensions and their significance in families lives. There is recent research literature which can be disseminated and integrated into training to help practitioners develop more culturally sensitive practice in order to meet the needs of all children appropriately.

The best solutions to needs will be best found through 'joined up' thinking and actions between agencies. Despite the overlapping knowledge base demonstrated in the literature, it appears that assessment information is not yet well integrated between agencies. Bureaucratic structural arrangements may have contributed to separating professionals who share similar concerns and goals for the welfare of children. Recent government initiatives provide an opportunity to change this.

The literature on the implementation of the NHS and Community Care Act 1990 considers some themes from which children and families workers can learn. The needs of vulnerable children are different from the needs of vulnerable adults. Children's needs are defined in a developmental way in the legislation and literature and so it may be more straightforward to relate a child's identified needs to the infra-structure of the child's family and community.

A shift in ideology

In order to implement the changes in assessment outlined above, ideological and structural shifts will be needed. A different mindset is needed from professionals. Reviewing literature on the American child welfare debate, Maluccio (1997, p. 140) suggests that 'most families coming to the attention of welfare agencies, with proper supports and services are capable of rearing their children'. This is congruent with British research in child protection (Department of Health, 1995). If so, targeting social work intervention through a structured inter-disciplinary approach could provide both a first-stop and last-stop assessment for most children, while for a few children at risk of significant harm or with more complex problems, more will always be needed. To implement a child centred approach, inter-disciplinary working will need to be strengthened, as suggested by recent central government initiatives, so that children's needs, in a holistic sense, can be properly addressed. This provides us, therefore, with a series of challenges.

The challenges

A rich and diverse literature is available from which a new approach to assessment can be constructed. Social workers need to implement a theory for practice which incorporates the following aspects:

- action and outcome based tools at all levels of assessment;

- a step by step approach (phased work) which shows:

    who is responsible?
    who will take action?
    who will evaluate?
    who will decide on the next step?
    what are the time limits?

- an approach which does not pathologise parents, but rather recognises what families should have, builds on parents' strengths, and uses a solution focused approach;

- an emphasis on reflective practice which balances risk and need in decision making;

- uses ecological perspectives to assess, but acts in relation to each specific need identified, by a range of interventions;

- seeks to support families by drawing strength from the community;

- has the capacity to monitor progress and review earlier assessment in the light of further assessment as changes happen;

- has the capacity to record and register unmet need;

- is thorough, but not overly time consuming (avoiding unmet need resulting in cycles of assessment without targeted intervention);

- is sufficiently discriminating; so that appropriate action is taken when a child is suffering or likely to suffer significant harm;

- provides a modular, targeted approach which allows subsequent assessment to be built on layers of assessments to be built on a foundation of information on children's development, parental capacity and strengths.

Endpiece

The way forward to a new framework for assessment is summed up by Weick and Saleeby (1995, p. 148), who also assert that 'the safety and security of all family members are always the first order of business.' They offer a vision of family support for the years ahead:

> As we move toward the 21st century, our policies for, theories about, and practice with families must be informed by our recognition of diverse family structures, the relationship between the family and community, and the capacities of families to sustain, survive and thrive in a world that does not always support their well-being… Family practice must validate family aspirations and provide members with expectations to achieve those aspirations… Social workers must share their rich understanding of families by proclaiming their strengths and by calling on communities to provide families with the resources they need. These responses are well fitted to the challenges of the coming century.

Bibliography

Abbott, A. (1995) 'Boundaries of social work or social work boundaries' *Social Services Review*, Dec. pp. 546-562, Chicago, University of Chicago.

Adcock, M. and White, R. (eds.) (1985) *Good Enough Parenting, A Framework for Assessment*, London, BAAF.

Adcock, M. and White, R. (eds.) (1997) *Significant Harm*, Croydon, Significant Publications.

Ahmed, S., Cheetham, J. and Small, J. (1986) *Social Work with Black Children and Their Families*, London, Batsford.

Aldgate, J., and Bradley, M. (1999) *Supporting Families Through Short Term Accommodation*, London, The Stationery Office.

Aldgate, J. and Colman, R. (1999) *Post Qualifying Conceptual Framework and Curriculum Guidance for the Advanced Childcare Award*, London, The Stationery Office.

★Aldgate, J. and Hill, M. (eds.) (1996) *Child Welfare Services, Developments in Law, Policy, Practice and Resarch*, London, Jessica Kingsley.

Aldgate, J. and Tunstill, J. (1996) *Making Sense of Section 17: Implementing Services for Children in Need within the 1989 Children Act*, London, HMSO.

Aldgate, J. and Tunstill, J. (1998) *Local Authority Prevention Under s17 for Children in Need, London*, The Stationery Office.

Allen-Meares, P. and Lane, B. A. (1987) 'Grounding social work practice in theory: ecosystems', *Social Casework: The Journal of Contemporary Social Work*, November, pp. 515-521.

★Anderson, S. C. (1995) 'Education for family centred practice', *Families in Society*, March, pp. 173-180.

Azzi-Lessing, L. J. and Allen, D. (1996) 'Assessing risk in families affected by substance abuse', *Child Abuse and Neglect*, 20 (9) September, pp. 833-842.

★Beardshaw, V. (1991) *Implementing Assessment and Care Management*, London, Kings Fund College Paper.

Bebbington, A. and Miles, J. (1989) 'The background of children who enter local authority care', *British Journal of Social Work*, 19 (5), pp. 349-368.

Bee, H. (1995) *The Developing Person*, sixth edition, London, Harper Row.

Belsky, J. (1993) Etiology of child maltreatment: a developmental – ecological analysis, *Psychological Bulletin*, 114 (3), pp. 413-434.

Bentovim, A., Gorell Barnes, G. and Cooklin, A. (1982), *Family Therapy: Complementary Frameworks of Theory and Practice*. Vols I and II, New York, Academic Press.

Bentovim, A. (1997), 'Significant harm in context', in M. Adcock and R. White (eds.) (1997) *Significant Harm*, Croydon, Significant Publications.

Beresford, B. (1995), *The Needs of Disabled Children and Their Families*, Social Policy Research Unit, University of York.

Birchall, E. and Hallett, C. (1995) *Working Together in Child Protection*, London, HMSO.

Black, D. (1990) 'What do children need from parents?' *Adoption and Fostering*, 14 (1), pp. 43-50.

Bowlby, J. (1988) *A Secure Base: Clinical Applications of Attachment Theory*, London, Routledge.

Bradford, J. (1995) *Caring for the Whole Child: a Holistic Approach to Spirituality*, London, The Children's Society.

Bradshaw, J. (1972) 'The concept of need', *New Society*, 30 March, pp. 640-643.

Brady, P. (1997) *Shaping Family Support: a study of specialist community based support for families of people with autistic spectrum disabilities, undertaken by the National Autistic Society*, London, National Autistic Society.

Brandon, M., Lewis, A., Thoburn J., and Way, A. (1999) *Safeguarding Children with the Children Act 1989*, London, The Stationery Office.

Brandon, M. and Lewis, A. (1996) 'Significant harm and children's experiences of domestic violence', *Child and Family Social Work*, 1 (1), pp. 33-42.

★Bray, S. and Preston-Shoot, M. (1995) *Empowering Practice in Social Care*, Milton Keynes, Open University Press.

Brearley, J. (1991) *Counselling and Social Work*, Buckingham, Open University Press.

★Browne, M. (1996) 'Needs assessment and community care', in J. Percy-Smith (ed.) *Needs Assessment in Public Policy*, Buckingham, Open University Press.

Bruner, J. S., Jolly, A. and Sylva, K. (1985) *Play, It's Role in Development and Evolution*, Harmondsworth, Penguin.

Cameron, H. (1997) *Early Infant Settlement – Research Implications*, paper to the Family Proceedings Conference, 12th December, Birmingham.

Campion, M. J. (1995) *Who's Fit to Be a Parent?*, London, Routledge.

Caplan, G. (1964) *Principles of Preventative Psychiatry*, New York, Basic Books.

Cicchetti, D. and Lynch, M. (1993) 'Towards an ecological / transactional model of community violence and child maltreatment, consequences for children's development', *Psychiatry*, (56), pp. 96-118.

Cicchetti, D. and Rizley, R. (1981) 'Developmental perspectives on the etiology, intergenerational transmission and sequelae of child maltreatment', *New Directions for Child Development* (11), pp. 31-55.

Cicchetti, D., Rogosch, F. A., Lynch, M. and Holt, K. D. (1993), 'Resilience in maltreated children: processes leading to adaptive outcome', *Development and Pyschopathology*, (5), pp. 629-647.

Cigno, K. and Bourn, D. (1998) (eds.) *Cognitive Behavioural Work in Practice*, Aldershot, Ashgate.

Cleaver, H. (1996) *Focus on Teenagers*, London, HMSO.

Cleaver, H., Unell, I. and Aldgate, J. (1999) *Children's Needs-Parental Capacity: the Impact of Parental Mental Illness, Problem Alcohol and Drug Use and Domestic Violence on Children's Development*, London, The Stationery Office .

★Cleaver, H., Wattam, C. and Cawson C. (1997) *Assessing Risk in Child Protection*, London, NSPCC.

★Cole, E. S. (1995), 'Becoming family centred, child welfare's challenge', *Families in Society*, March, pp. 163-172.

Compton, B. R. and Galaway, B. (1989) *Social Work Processes*, Pacific Grove, Brookes Cole.

Connolly, J. and Shemmings, D. (1998) *Undertaking Assessments of Children and Families: a Directory of Training Materials Courses and Key Texts for Professionals*, Norwich, University of East Anglia.

Coombe, V. and Little, A. (eds.) (1986) *Race and Social Work: a Guide to Training*, London, Tavistock.

Corby, B. (1996) 'Risk assessment in child protection' in H. Kemshall and J. Pritchard (eds.) (1996) *Good Practice in Risk Assessment and Risk Management*, London, Jessica Kingsley.

Coulshed, V. (1991) *Social Work Practice: an Introduction*, London, MacMillan.

Courtney, M. E., Barth, R. P., Berrick, J. D., Brooks, D., Needell, B. and Park, L. (1996) 'Race and child welfare services: past research and future directions', *Child Welfare*, 75 (2) March/April pp. 99-132.

Crompton, M. (1996) (ed.) *Children Spirituality and Religion*, London CCETSW.

Curnock, K. and Hardiker, P. (1979) *Towards Practice Theory, Skills and Methods in Social Assessments*, London, Routledge, Kegan and Paul.

Curtis, S. (ed.) (1986) *From Asthma to Thalassaemia*, London, British Agencies for Adoption and Fostering.

Dale, N. (1996) *Working With Families of Children With Special Needs: Partnership and Practice*, London, Routledge.

Dalgleish, L. I. and Drew, E. C. (1989) 'The relationship of child abuse indicators to the assessment of perceived risk and to the court's decision to separate', *Child Abuse and Neglect*, (13), pp. 491-506.

Dalgleish, L. I. (1997) *Risk Assessment Approaches: The Good, the Bad and the Ugly*, paper to the Sixth Australasian Conference on Child Abuse and Neglect, 20-24th October, Adelaide, South Australia.

Dalgleish, L. I. (1999) *Risk Assessment and Decision Making in Child Protection*, London, Wiley.

David, T. (ed.) (1994) *Protecting Children from Abuse: Multi-Professionalism and the Children Act 1989*, London, Trentham Books.

Deakin, N. (1996) 'Contracting and accountability: the British experience', in H.J. Schulze and W. With (eds.) *Who Cares: Social Service Organisations and Their Users*, London, Cassell.

Department of Health, (1988) *Protecting Children: A Guide for Social Workers Undertaking a Comprehensive Assessment*, London, HMSO.

Department of Health, (1991a) *Assessment Systems and Community Care*, London, HMSO.

Department of Health, (1991b) *Care Management and Assessment: Practitioners Guide*, London, HMSO.

Department of Health, (1991c) *Child Abuse, A Study of Inquiry Reports 1980-9*, London, HMSO.

Department of Health, (1995) *Child Protection Messages from Research*, London, HMSO.

Department of Health, (1998) *Working Together to Safeguard Children: New Government Proposals for Inter-agency Co-operation*, London, The Stationery Office.

Department of Health, (1999) *Assessing Children in Need and Their Families*, London, The Stationery Office.

Department of Health and Cleaver, H. (1999) Work in Progress.

De Shazer, S. (1985) *Keys to Solution in Brief Therapy*, New York, Norton.

De Winter, M. (ed.) (1997) *Children as Fellow Citizens*, London, Radcliffe Medical Press.

Doel, M. and Marsh P. (1992) *Task Centred Social Work*, Aldershot, Arena.

Doueck, H. J., Bronson, D. E. and Levine, M. (1992) 'Evaluating risk assessment implementation in child protection: issues for consideration', *Child Abuse and Neglect*, 16, pp. 637-646.

Dowie, J. and Elstein, A. (eds.) (1988) *Professional Judgement: A Reader in Clinical Judgement Making*, Cambridge, Cambridge University Press.

Doyal, L. and Gough, I. (1991) *A Theory of Human Need*, London, MacMillan.

Dungee-Anderson, D. and Beckett, J. O. (1995) 'A process model for multicultural social work practice', *Families in Society*, October, pp. 459-467.

Dunn, J. (1984) *Brothers and Sisters*, London, Fontana.

Dunn, J. (1993) *Young Children's Close Relationships*, London, Sage.

Dutt, R. and Phillips, M. (1999) *Department of Health Needs Led Assessment of Children and Families – Suggested Framework and Content of REU's Contribution*, Working Paper for the Department of Health, Race Equality Unit.

Edwards, J. (1995) 'Parenting skills : views of community health and social services providers about the needs of their clients', *The Journal of Social Policy*, 24 (2) pp. 237-259.

Egan, G. (1990) *The Skilled Helper*, Pacific Grove, California, Brooks/Cole.

Einion, D. (1985) *Creative Play*, London, Viking.

English, D. and Pecora, P. (1994) 'Risk assessment as a practice in child protection services', *Child Welfare*, (53) pp. 451-473.

Epstein, L. (1988) *Helping People: The Task Centred Approach*, 2nd ed. Columbus Ohio, C. E. Merrill.

Erickson, G. D. and Hogan, T. (1972) *Family Therapy: An Introduction to Theory and Technique*, Belmont, Wadsworth.

Erikson, E. (1965) *Childhood and Society*, Harmondsworth, Penguin.

Erwin, P. (1993) *Friendship and Peer Relations in Children*, London, Wiley.

Fahlberg, V. (1981) *Attachment and Separation*, London, BAAF.

Fahlberg, V. (1982) *Child Development*, London, BAAF.

Fairbairn, W. R. D. (1952) *Psychoanalytic Studies of the Personality*, London, Routledge and Kegan Paul.

Farmer, E. and Owen, M. (1995) *Child Protection Practice: Private Risks and Public Remedies*, London, HMSO.

Farrell, P. (1995) *Children with Emotional and Behavioural Difficulties: Strategies for Assessment and Intervention*, London, The Falmer Press.

Flaks, D. K., Joseph, G., Masterpaqua, F. and Fischer, I. (1995) 'Lesbians choosing motherhood: a comparative study of lesbian and heterosexual parents and their children', *Developmental Psychology*, 31(1) January, pp. 105-114.

Flekkoy, M. G. (1991) *A Voice for Children*, London, Jessica Kingsley.

Fraiberg, S. (1959, reprinted 1995) *The Magic Years*, Scribner.

Franklin, C. and Jordan, C. (1995) 'Qualitative assessment: a methological review', *Families in Society*, May, pp. 281-295.

Friel, J. (1995) *Children With Special Needs: Assessment, Law and Practice 'Caught in the Acts'*, London, Jessica Kingsley.

Frost, (1997) 'Delivering family support: issues and themes in service development,' in N. Parton (ed.) *Child Protection and Family Support, Tensions, Contradictions and Possibilities*, London, Routledge.

Gaffney, M. (1998) *Assessing Younger Children and Families: a Whale by the Tail*, London, NCH.

Garborino, J. (1982) *Children and Families in the Social Environment*, New York, Aldine.

Gaudin, J. M., Shilton, P., Kilpatrick, A. C., and Polansky, N. A. (1996) 'Family functioning in neglectful families', *Child Abuse and Neglect*, 20 (4) April, pp. 363-377.

★Gibbons, J. (1990) *Family Support and Prevention: Studies in Local Areas*, London, HMSO.

Gilligan, R. (1997) 'Beyond permanence, the importance of resilience in child placement practice and planning', *Adoption and Fostering*, 21 (1), pp. 13-19.

Gitterman, A. (1996), 'Debate with authors: ecological perspective: response to Professor Jerry Wakefield', *Social Sciences Review*, 70 (3), pp. 473-477.

Goddard, A. and Powell, J. (1996) 'Cost and stakeholder views: a combined approach to evaluating services', *British Journal of Social Work*, 26 (1), pp. 93-108.

Golan, N. (1981) *Passing Through Transitions*, London, Collier-Macmillan.

★Goldstein, B. D. (1995) 'The who, what, when, where, and why of risk characterisation', *Policy Studies Journal*, 23 (1) Spring, pp. 70-75.

Gorrell Barnes, G. (1994) 'Family Therapy', in M. Rutter, E. Taylor and L. Hersov L. (eds.) *Child and Adolescent Psychiatry: Modern Approaches*, (3rd ed), pp. 946-967, London, Blackwell.

Guralnick, M. J. (1997) (ed.) *The Effectiveness of Early Intervention*, London, Brookes/Cole.

Hagell, A. (1998) *Dangerous Care, Reviewing the Risks to Children from their Carers*, London, The Bridge.

Haines, J. (1975) *Skills and Methods in Social Work*, London, Constable.

Hallett, C. and Birchall, E. (1995) *Co-ordination and Child Protection*, Edinburgh, HMSO.

Hamilton, M. A. and Orme, J. G. (1990) 'Examining the construct validity of three parenting knowledge measures using LISREL', *Social Service Review*, March, pp. 120-143.

★Hardiker, P. and Barker, M. (eds.) (1981) *Theories of Practice in Social Work*, London, Academic Press.

Hardiker, P. and Barker, M. (1991) 'Towards social theory for social work', in J. Lishman (ed.) *Handbook of Theory for Practice Teachers in Social Work*, pp 87-119, London, Jessica Kingsley.

Hardiker, P. and Barker, M. (1994) *The 1989 Children Act - Significant Harm, The Experience of Social Workers Implementing New Legislation*, Leicester, University of Leicester School of Social Work.

Hardiker, P. and Barker, M. (1996) *The NHS and Community Care Act 1990: Needs-led Assessments and Packages of Care*, Leicester, University of Leicester School of Social Work.

Hardiker, P., Exton, K. and Barker, M. (1996) 'A framework for analysing services', *Childhood Matters*: Vol 2: Background Papers, London, HMSO.

Hardiker, P., Seden, J. and Barker, M. (1995) 'Children first: protection and prevention in services for disabled children, Part I', *Child Care in Practice*, 2 (1) September, pp. 1-17.

Hardiker, P., Seden, J. and Barker, M. (1995) Children first: protection and prevention in services for disabled children, Part II, *Child Care in Practice*, 2 (2) December, pp. 1-9.

Hasenfeld, Y. S. (1993) *Human Services Organisations*, Eaglewoods Cliffs, Prentice Hall.

Hawkins, P. and Shohet, R. (1989) *Supervision in the Helping Professions*, Buckingham, Open University Press.

Hemming, K., Leitenberg, H., Coffey, P., Bennett, T. and Jankowski, M. (1997) 'Long-term psychological adjustment to witnessing interparental physical conflict during childhood', *Child Abuse and Neglect*, 21 (6), pp. 501-516.

Herbert, M. (1981) *Behavioural Treatment of Problem Children, A Practice Manual*, London, Academic Press.

Herbert, M., (1987) *Living With Teenagers*, London, Blackwell.

Herbert, M. (1989) *Discipline*, London, Blackwell.

Herbert, M. (1997) *Working with Children and the Children Act*. Leicester BPS Books.

Hoffman, L. (1981) *The Foundations of Family Therapy*, New York, Basic Books.

Hollin, C. (1990) *Cognitive Behavioural Intervention wih Young Offenders*, Oxford, Pergamon Press.

Hollis, F. (1964) *Casework: a Psycho-social Therapy*, New York, Random House.

Holt, K. S. (1991) *Child Development: Diagnosis and Assessment*, Rushden, Butterworth/Heinemann.

Home Office (1997) *Management and Assessment of Risk in the Probation Service*, London, The Stationery Office.

Home Office, (1998) *Report of the What Works Project: Strategies for Effective Offender Supervision*, London, The Stationery Office.

Howe, D. (1987) *An Introduction to Social Work Theory*, Aldershot, Wildwood House.

Howe, D. (1995) *Attachment Theory for Social Work Practice*, Basingstoke, MacMillan.

Howlin, P. and Jones, P. H. (1996) 'An assessment approach to abuse allegations made through facilitated communication', *Child Abuse and Neglect*, 20 (2), pp. 103-110.

Hudson, B. L. and MacDonald, G. M. (1986) *Behavioural Social Work: an Introduction*, London, Routledge.

Hudson, B. L. (1991) 'Behavioural social work', in J. Lishman (ed.) *Handbook of Theory for Practice Teachers in Social Work*, pp. 123-137, London, Jessica Kingsley.

Humphries, B. (1996) *Critical Perspectives on Empowerment*, Birmingham, Ventura Press.

★International Initiative Seminar Report, The (1997) *Seminar, Protecting Children by Strengthening Families*, Leicester, International Initiative, UK.

Iwaniec, D. (1995) *The Emotionally Abused and Neglected Child; Identification, Assessment and Intervention*, London, Wiley.

Jack, G. (1996) 'An ecological approach to social work with children and their families', *Child and Family Social Work*, (2) pp. 109-120, Oxford, Blackwells.

Jehu, D. (1992) 'Adult survivors of sexual abuse', in R.T. Ammermen and M. Hersen (eds.) *Assessment of Family Violence: a Clinical and Legal Sourcebook*, New York, Wiley.

Jones, D. P. H. (1997), 'The effectiveness of intervention' in M. Adcock and R. White (eds.) (1997) *Significant Harm*, Croydon, Significant Publications.

Jones, D. P. H. and Ramchandi, P. (1999) *Child Sexual Abuse, Informing Practice from Research*, Oxford, Radcliffe Medical Press.

Kadushin, A. (1997) *Supervision in Social Work*, New York, Columbia University Press.

Katz, L., Spoonemore, N. and Robinson, C. (1994) *Concurrent Planning: From Permanency Planning to Permanency Action*, Washington, Lutheran Social Services.

Kaufman Kantor, G. and Jasinski, J. L. (1997) *Out of the Darkness, Contemporary Perspectives on Family Violence*, London, Sage.

★Kelly, N. and Milner, J. (1996) 'Child protection decision making', *Child Abuse Review*, 5 (2), pp. 91-102.

Kelmer Pringle, M. (1980) *The Needs of Children*, London, Hutchinson.

Kemshall, H. (1995) 'Risks in probation practice: the hazards and dangers of supervision' *Probation Journal*, 42 (2) June, pp. 67-72.

Kemshall, H. (1996) 'Risk assessment: fuzzy thinking or decisions in action' *Probation Journal*, 43 (1) April, pp. 2-7.

Kemshall, H. and Pritchard, J. (1996) (eds.) *Good Practice in Risk Assessment and Risk Management*, London, Jessica Kingsley.

Knutsson, K. E. (1997) *Children, Noble Causes or Worthy Citizens?*, Florence, Arena and UNICEF.

Lago, C. and Thompson, J. (1996) *Race, Culture and Counselling*, Buckingham, Open University Press.

Laird, J. (1995) 'Family centred practice in the postmodern era', *Families in Society*, March, pp. 150-162.

Lamb, M. E. (1997) *The Role of the Father in Child Development*, London, Wiley.

Lau, M. (1984), 'Transcultural issues in family therapy', *Journal of Family Therapy*, (6), pp. 91-112.

*Leicestershire County Council, (1996) *Community Care: Practice Guidance*, Leicestershire Social Services Information Services, Glenfield, Leicester.

Lhullier, J. M. and Martin, C. (1994) 'Social work at the turn of the century', *Social Policy and Administration*, 28 (1), pp. 359-69

Lindon, J. (1996) *Child Development from Birth to Eight*, London, National Childrens Bureau.

Lindsey, D. (1994), *The Welfare of Children*, Oxford, University Press.

*Lipsky, M. (1980) *Street Level Bureaucracy*, New York, Sage.

Lishman, J. (1991) (ed.) *Handbook of Theory for Practice Teachers in Social Work*, London, Jessica Kingsley.

Lloyd, M. and Taylor, C. (1995) 'From Hollis to the orange book', *British Journal of Social Work*, 25 (6), pp. 691-707.

London Borough of Brent, (1985) *A Child in Trust: report of the panel of inquiry investigating the circumstances surrounding the death of Jasmine Beckford*, London, Borough of Brent.

Lyons, P., Wodarski, J. S. and Doueck, H. J. (1996) 'Risk assessment for child protective services: a review of the empirical literature on instrument performance', *Social Work Research*, 20 (3) September, pp. 143-155.

McGuire, J. (1995) (ed.) *What Works: Reducing Offending: Guidelines from Research and Practice*, Chicester, Wiley.

Maluccio, A. (ed.) (1981) *Promoting Competence in Clients: a New/Old Approach to Social Work Practice*, New York, The Free Press.

Maluccio, A. (1997) 'Time for an ideological shift in child welfare? An essay review', *Social Service Review*, March, pp. 136-141.

Marsh, P. and Triseliotis, J. (1996) *Ready to Practise? Social Workers and Probation Officers: Their Training and First Year in Work*, Aldershot, Avebury.

Maslow, A. H. (1943) 'A theory of human motivation', *Psychological Review*, 50, pp. 370-378.

*May, J. (ed.) (1996) *Children in Charge, the Child's Right to a Fair Hearing*, London, Jessica Kingsley.

Mayer, J. E. and Timms, N. (1970) *The Client Speaks*, London, Routledge, Kegan and Paul.

Meyer, C. H. (1993) *Assessment in Social Work*, New York, Columbia University Press.

Miller, I. W., Kabacoff, R. I., Epstein, N. B., Bishop, D. S., Keitner, G. I., Baldwin, L. M. and Van der Spuy, H. I. J. (1994) 'The development of a clinical rating scale for the McMaster model of family functioning', *Family Process*, 33 (1) March, pp. 53-65.

Minuchin, S. (1974) *Families and Family Therapy*, Tavistock, London.

Modernising Social Services: Promoting independence; Improving Protection; Raising Standards (1988) Cm4169. London, The Stationery Office.

Mooney, A. and Munton, A. G. (1997) *Research and Policy in Early Childhood Services: Time for a New Agenda*. London Institute of Education, University of London.

Moss, P. and Petrie, P. (1996) *Time for a New Approach: a Discussion Paper*, London, Thomas Coram Research Unit.

Murphy, M. (1993) *Working Together in Child Protection: an Exploration of the Multi-disciplinary Task and System*, Ashgate, Arena.

Murphy-Berman, V. (1994) 'A conceptual framework for thinking about risk assessment and case management in child protective services', *Child Abuse and Neglect*, 18 (2) February, pp. 193-201.

Murray, L. and Cooper, P. J. (1997) 'Post partum depression and child development', *Psychological Medicine*, 27 pp. 253-260 Cambridge University Press.

Mussen, P. H., Conger J., Kagan, J. and Huston, A. C. (1990) *Child Development and Personality*, (7th ed), London, Harper and Row.

National Foster Care Association Publications (1998).

NCH Action for Children – Cymru, (1997) *Practice Guidance: Working with Children and Young People who Sexually Abuse Others*, Cardiff, NCH.

NSPCC, (1997) *Turning Points: a Resource Pack for Communicating with Children*, Leicester, NSPCC with Chailey Heritage and the Department of Health.

Nelson, D. (1997) 'The building blocks of neighbourhoods that support families,' (in press).

Neville, D., Beak, D. and King, L. (1996) *Positive Parenting*, Ashgate, Arena.

Neville, D., Beak, D. and King, L. (1998) *Positive Parenting with Teenagers*, Aldershot, Gower.

O'Hagan, K. P. (1986) *Crisis Intervention in Social Services*, London, Macmillan.

Paquin, G. W. and Bushorn, R. J. (1991) 'Family treatment, assessment for novices', *Families in Society*, June, pp. 353-359.

Parker, R., Ward H., Jackson S., Aldgate, J. and Wedge P. (eds.) (1991) *Assessing Outcomes in Child Care*, London, HMSO.

Parkes, C. M., Stevenson-Hinde, J. and Morris, P. (1991) *Attachment Across the Life Cycle*, London, Routledge.

Parton, N. (ed.) (1997) *Child Protection and Family Support*, London, Routledge.

Payne, M. (1992) *Modern Social Work Theory: a Critical Introduction*, London, MacMillan.

Pearson, G. (ed.) (1988) *Social Work and the Legacy of Freud*, London, Macmillan.

Pederson, P. B. (1997) *Culture Centred Counselling Interventions: Striving for Accuracy*, London, Sage.

★Peel, M. (1996) *Refocussing Children's Services Initiative: Literature Review*, University of Leicester.

Percy-Smith, J. (ed.) (1996) *Needs Assessments in Public Policy*, Buckingham, Open University Press.

Perry, B. D. (1993) 'Neuro-development and the neuro-physiology of trauma', *The Advisor*, 6 (1) pp 1, 14-18 and 6 (2) pp. 1, 14-20.

Phoenix, A., Woolett, A. and Lloyd E. (eds.) (1991) *Motherhood: Meanings, Practices and Ideologies*, London, Sage.

Pincus, A. and Minahan, A. (1973) *Social Work Practice: Model and Method*, Itasca, Peacock.

Pinderhughes, E. (1995) 'Empowering diverse populations: family practice in the 21st century,' *Families in Society*, March, pp. 131-140.

Pittman, F. S. (1966) 'Techniques of family crisis therapy' in J. Masserman (ed.) *Current Psychiatric Therapies*, New York, Grune and Stratton.

Powell, J. and Goddard, A. (1996) 'Cost and stakeholder views: a combined approach to evaluating services,' *British Journal of Social Work*, 26 (1) February, pp. 93-108.

Prins, H. (1995) 'Seven sins of omission', *Probation Journal*, 42 (4) December, pp. 199-201.

Pugh, G. (ed.) (1992) *Contemporary Issues in the Early Years, Working Collaboratively for Children*, London, National Childrens Bureau.

Puttnam, F. (1998) *The Effect of Maltreatment on Early Brain Development*, APSAC Conference, January.

Reder, P., Duncan, S. and Gray, M. (1993) *Beyond Blame: Child Abuse Tragedies Revisited*, London, Routledge.

Reder, P. and Lucey, C. (1995) *Assessment of Parenting: Psychiatric and Psychological Contributions*, London, Routledge.

Reid, W. J. (1963) *An Experimental Study of Methods Used in Casework Treatment*, New York, Columbia University PhD. Dissertation.

Reid, W. J. and Epstein, L. (1972) *Task-centred Casework*, New York, Columbia University Press.

Reid, W. J. and Epstein, L. (1976) *Task-centred Practice*, New York, Columbia University Press.

Reid, W. J. and Shyne, A. W. (1969) *Brief and Extended Casework*, New York, Columbia University Press.

Richmond, M. E. (1922) *Social Diagnosis*, New York, Russell Sage Foundation.

Roberts, R. (1990) *Lessons From the Past: Issues for Social Work Theory*, London, Routledge.

Roberts, R. W. and Nee, R. H. (eds.) (1980) *Theories of Social Casework*, Chicago, University of Chicago Press.

Rogers, C. R. (1961) *On Becoming a Person*, Boston, Houghton Mifflin.

★Rollnick, M. W. (1996) *Motivational Interviewing*, London, Guildford Press.

Roner, T. (1993) Adapting Treatment Techniques to Children's Needs, *British Journal of Social Work*, 23, pp. 551-596.

Rosenstein, P. (1995) 'Parental levels of empathy as related to risk assessment in child protective services,' *Child Abuse and Neglect*, 19 (11) November, pp. 1349-1360.

Rowntree Foundation, (1998) *Disabled Children and the Children Act*.

Russell, P. (1997) 'Children with disabilities' in H. Kemshall and J. Pritchard (eds.) *Good Practice in Risk Assessment and Risk Management*, London, Jessica Kingsley.

Rutter, M. (1981) *Maternal Deprivation Re-assessed*, (2nd ed.), Harmondsworth, Penguin.

Rutter, M. (1985), 'Resilience in the face of adversity: protective factors and resilience to psychiatric disorder', *British Journal of Psychiatry*, 147, pp. 163-182.

Rutter, M., Taylor, E. and Hersov, L. (1994) *Child and Adolescent Psychiatry: Modern Approaches*, (3rd ed), London, Blackwell.

Rutter, M. (ed.) (1995) *Psychosocial Disturbances in Young People: Challenges for Prevention*, Cambridge, Cambridge University Press.

★Sainsbury, E. (ed.) *Working with Children in Need, Studies in Complexity and Challenge*, London, Jessica Kingsley.

Saleebey, D. (1997) *The Strengths Perspective in Social Work Practice*, New York, Longman.

Scannapieco, M. and Hegar, R. L. (1996) 'A non-traditional assessment framework for formal kinship homes' *Child Welfare*, 57 (5), pp. 566-579.

Schaffer, R. H. (1977) *Mothering*, London, Fontana.

Schaffer, R. H. (1990) *Making Decisions about Children, Psychological Questions and Answers*, Oxford, Blackwell.

Schon, D. (1983) *The Reflective Practitioner*, New York, Basic Books.

Scott, D. and O'Neill, D. (1996) *Beyond Child Rescue: Developing Family-Centred Practice at St Lukes*, St Leonards, Allen and Unwin.

Scott, M. (1983) *Group Parent Training Programme Programme*, Liverpool Personal Service Society.

Scott, M. (1989) *A Cognitive Approach to Clients' Problems*, London, Routledge.

Seden, J. (1995) 'Religious persuasion and the Children Act', *Adoption and Fostering*, 19 (2), pp. 7-15.

Sheldon, B. (1995) *Cognitive Behaviour Therapy: Research, Practice and Philosophy*, London, Routledge.

Sheldon, B. (1982) *Behaviour Modification: Theory, Practice and Philosophy*, London, Tavistock.

Sheppard, M. (1993) 'Maternal depression and child care: the significance for social work and social work research', *Adoption and Fostering*, 17 (2), pp. 10-16.

Sheridan, M. (1997) *From Birth to Five Years* (revised and updated), London, Routledge.

★Sheridan, M. J. (1995) 'A psychometric assessment of the children of alcoholics screening test (CAST)', *Journal of Studies on Alcohol*, 56 (2) March, pp. 156-160.

Sinclair, R., Garnett, L. and Berridge, D. (1995) *Social Work and Assessment with Adolescents*, London, National Children's Bureau.

Sinclair, R. Hearn, B. and Pugh, G. (1997) *Preventive Work with Families: The Role of Mainstream Services*, London, National Children's Bureau

Siporin, M. (1975) *Introduction to Social Work Practice*, New York Macmillan.

Skellington, R. and Morris, P. (1992) *Race in Britain Today*, London, Sage and the Open University.

Skuse, D. and Bentovim, A. (1994) 'Physical and emotional maltreatment' in M. Rutter, E. Taylor and L. Hersov (1994) *Child and Adolescent Psychiatry: Modern Approaches*, (3rd ed.), London, Blackwell.

Sloper, T. (1997) Conference presentation: *Messages from Research*, York, Social Policy Research Unit.

Solomon, B. (1976) *Black Empowerment: Social Work in Oppressed Communities*, New York, Colombia University Press.

Specht, H. and Vickery, A. (1977) *Integrating Social Work Methods*, London, George, Allen and Unwin.

★Stern, S. B. and Smith, C. A. (1995) 'Family process and delinquency in an ecological context' *Social Service Review*, December, pp. 703-730.

Stevenson, O. (1998) *Neglected Children: Issues and Dilemmas*, Oxford, Blackwell.

Sylva, S. and Lunt, I. (1995) *Child Development: a First Course*, Oxford, Blackwell.

Taylor, B. and Devine, T. (1993) *Assessing Needs and Planning Care*, Aldershot, Arena.

★Taylor-Gooby, P. and Lawson, R. (eds.) (1993) *Markets and Managers: New Issues in the Delivery of Welfare*, Buckingham, Open University Press.

★Thompson, N. (1995) *Aging with Dignity*, Ashgate, Arena.

Thoburn. J., Lewis, A. and Shemmings, D. (1995) *Paternalism or Partnership? Family Involvement in the Child Protection Process*, London, HMSO.

Tizard, B. and Phoenix, A. (1993) *Black, White or Mixed Race?*, London, Routledge.

Trowell, J. and Bower, M. (1996) *The Emotional Needs of Young Children and Their Families*, London, Routledge.

★Trowell, J, Hodges, S. and Leighton-Lang, J. (1977) 'The work of a family centre', *Child Abuse Review*, (6), pp. 357-369.

Tunstill J. and Aldgate J. (1999) *Children in Need from Policy to Practice*, London, The Stationery Office.

★Usher, C. L., Gibbs, D. A. and Wildfire, J. B. (1995) 'A framework for planning, implementing and evaluating child welfare reform', *Child Welfare*, 54 (4), pp. 859-876.

Valente, M. (1998) 'Child protection and inter-agency working: a discussion', *Practice*, Vol 10 (3) pp. 37-43.

Van der Eyken, W., Williams, S. and Vallender, I. (1997) *Finding Out: an Informal Guide to Self-evaluation for Family Centres*, London, National Council for Voluntary Child Care Organisations.

Victoria Youth and Family Services, (1997) *The Redevelopment of Victoria's Youth and Family Services, Strategic Directions*.

Wakefield, J. (1996), 'Does social work need the eco-systems perspective?' (1) and (2), *Social Services Review*, 70 (1) March, pp. 1-32, and 70 (4) June. pp. 183-213.

Wald, M. and Woolverton, M. (1990) 'Risk assessment: the emperor's new clothes?' *Child Welfare*, 69, pp. 483-511.

Walrond-Skinner, S. (1976) *Family Therapy, the Treatment of Natural Systems*, Routledge and Kegan Paul, London.

Ward, H. (1995) *Looking After Children, Assessing Outcomes*, London, HMSO.

Weick, A. and Saleebey, D. (1995) 'Supporting family strengths: orienting policy and practice towards the 21st century', *Families in Society*, March, pp. 141-149.

Westcott, H. L. (1992) 'The abuse of disabled children: a review of the literature, *Child Care Health and Development*, 17, pp. 243-258.

Westcott, H. L. (1992) 'The cognitive interview a useful tool for social workers?', *British Journal of Social Work*, 22, pp. 519-533.

Whalley, M. (1994) *Learning to be Strong: Setting up a Neighbourhood Service for Under Fives and their Families*, Sevenoaks, Hodder and Stoughton.

White, M. and Epston, D. (1989) *Narrative Means to Therapeutic Ends*, New York, Norton.

Widom, C. S. (1996) 'Understanding the consequences of childhood victimisation,' manuscript submitted to the *American Journal of Orthopsychiatry*.

Will, D. and Wrate, R. M. (1985) *Integrated Family Therapy*, London, Tavistock.

Winnicott, D. W. (1960) 'The theory of the parent-infant relationship', *International Journal of Psycho-analysis*, 41, pp. 585-595.

Winnicott, D. W. (1964) *The Child the Family and the Outside World*, London, Penguin.

Winnicott, D. W. (1986) *Home is Where We Start From*, Harmondsworth, Penguin.

★Woodhead, M., Light, P. and Carr, R. (1991) *Growing Up in a Changing Society*, Buckingham, Open University Press.

Yelloly, M. (1980) *Social Work Theory and Psychoanalysis*, New York, Van Nostrand.

Yelloly, M. and Henkel, M. (eds.) (1995) *Learning and Teaching in Social Work: Towards Reflective Practice*, London, Jessica Kingsley.

References marked ★ are not cited in the text but are valuable reading.

Study B

The Language of need: social workers describing the needs of children

Ruth Sinclair

Study B: Contents

Acknowledgements

The project team would like to thank all the local authority social workers who participated in the project work by allowing their case files to be scrutinised by the team and giving their time for interviews.

Project Team

Andrea Hickman	Project Leader, Central Social Care Region, Department of Health
Jenny Gray	Social Care Group 3, Department of Health
John Rowlands	Social Care Group 3, Department of Health
Jennifer Ruddick	Southern Social Care Region, Department of Health
Ruth Sinclair	Project report writer, National Children's Bureau

December 2000

Introduction

Before it is possible to meet the needs of children it is first necessary to identify those needs and to make a record of them. This means describing the needs of individual children, and doing so accurately, comprehensively and in a way that has meaning to others. Understanding the manner in which social workers describe the needs of children is important at two levels: first at the level of the individual case, it illuminates the assessment process and as such can help in developing tools to enhance the standards of assessment. Second at a service level, if the needs of children can be described in a way that is capable of aggregation into meaningful categories this can assist in planning services to respond to those needs. These represent two very different end purposes. Nonetheless it may be possible to meet both these purposes starting from the same information source. That was certainly the hope of the project reported here.

An exercise was designed to explore more fully the language used by social workers to describe the needs of the children with whom they are working. More specifically the exercise set out to:

- identify the actual words and phrases that social workers use to describe the needs of children on their caseloads, and to analyse the nature of these descriptions;

- consider how comprehensively social workers describe the needs of children, using the seven dimensions of the *Looking After Children* materials;

- test again the categorisation of the causes of need used previously in the Mori/York/NCB study (See Appendix 1).

From this it was hoped to identify first if there was any pattern to the described needs of children that suggested clear groupings of children and second if there was any pattern to the language that social workers used to describe similar needs.

1 Methods

Interviews were undertaken with social workers in respect of 40 different children with whom they were currently working. The interviews were conducted by four SSI inspectors in four different local authorities. During these interviews social workers were asked to describe the needs of each child using three different frameworks:

- by describing freely, without any structure and minimal prompting, what they saw as the needs of the child;

- using the seven developmental dimensions of the *Looking After Children* materials, plus an additional eighth – significant harm – to consider needs under each of these headings and to say whether they saw each of these areas of need as a high, medium or low priority;

- using the eightfold categorisation of the causes of need arising from the Mori/York/NCB work to say for each case if a particular category was a contributory cause of need, and if more than one applied which was the principal cause of need.

The interview schedule is included as appendix 2.

The interviews were taped and transcribed and analysed with use of QSR Nud*ist software. Although there are indications of some variations between the four interviewers in the manner in which the questions were posed, this is not felt to impact upon the particular analysis presented in this report.

The sample of cases

The cases in the sample were chosen from the case loads of selected social workers in four authorities. A sample of 40 cases was selected to include children in need including disabled children, children whose names were on the

Child Protection Register and children looked after. The characteristics of the sample are described below using six variables: age and sex; ethnic origin; legal status; current placement and type of case.

Table B.1: *Age and sex*

Age	Males	Females	Totals	%
under 1 year	2	0	2	5.0
1–5 years	3	5	8	20.0
1–10 years	6	3	9	22.5
11–15 years	11	5	16	40.0
16+	2	3	5	12.5
Totals	24	16	40	
%	60.0	40.0	100.0	100.0

There was no national data on 'children in need' with which the sample could be compared. A comparison with the age structure of the child population taken from the 1991 census shows the sample to be reasonably representative; the most noticeable difference being in the larger proportion of 10 -14 children in the sample (see Table B.1a below) . The age distribution of the sample is closer to that of the national 'children looked after' population which also has a high proportion of adolescents.

Table B.1a: *Age structures*

Age group	Sample	1991 census
0-1	5.0	5.4
1-4	15.0	20.9
5-9	20.0	24.8
10 -14	35.0	23.7
15-19	25.0	5.3

Table B.2: *Ethnic Origin*

	No.	%
White	28	70.0
Black	2	5.0
Asian	0	0.0
Mixed Parentage	3	7.5
Not recorded	7	17.5
	40	100.0

Unfortunately no information on ethnic origin was available for a substantial group of children (18% of the sample). This makes it difficult to comment on the proportions overall, except to note that in line with other statistical reports the largest group of children from minority ethnic groups is those of mixed parentage.

Table B.3: *Legal / Administrative Status*

	No.	%
S17 (only)	15	37.5
S20	11	27.5
ICO	2	5.0
CO	9	22.5
CPR (only)	2	5.0
SO	1	2.5
	40	100.0

A substantial proportion (38%) of the sample were not on any statutory order but were receiving support through an allocated social worker, sometimes attached to a specialist team.

Table B.4: *Placement*

	No.	%
Home	17	42.5
Extended Family	4	10.0
Foster Care	13	32.5
Residential Care	3	7.5
Residential School	2	5.0
Semi-independent	1	2.5
	40	100.0

More than half the sample were living at home or with extended family members.

Table B.5: *Type of Cases*

	No.	%
Child Protection	13	32.5
Likely to be accommodated	4	10.0
Children in need	3	7.5
Looked after	8	20.0
Disabled	6	15.0
Beyond control	5	12.5
Leaving care	1	2.5
	40	100.0

2 *The Descriptions of Need*

Social workers were asked to describe freely what they saw as the needs of each child, with minimal prompting from the interviewer. In the main the social workers had little difficulty applying a needs-focused analysis to their cases; in only a small number of instances did respondents demonstrate an inability to move beyond a descriptive account of behaviours and events to apply a more analytical framework of either underlying causes of need or the manifestations of need arising from particular presenting problems.

The interview transcripts were scrutinised to identify the sorts of words, phrases, sentences that social workers used to describe needs. The important direct quotes from each case were subsequently used as the basis of analysis. Inevitably in interview it was often necessary for the social worker to provide some contextual or background information on the case in order to make sense of current needs. In general these were not included, unless they offer necessary succinct explanation of the context of the assessment of needs. While descriptions of need were presented at all three stages of this exercise the discussion here relates to the direct quotations taken largely, but not exclusively, from the first unstructured component.

These descriptions of need are considered in more detail below in respect of their comprehensiveness and the type of needs that are identified. But first there are some broader issues raised by this exercise.

- *Which needs apply, when:* the interviews demonstrate the evolving nature of some needs as circumstances in the child's life change and hence the importance of marking the point in time to which the described needs are applicable – at point of referral, currently, likely to arise in the future. This is important in terms of review and re-assessment of needs and service provision; it is also important in respect of the image of the child that workers carry in their heads. They need to ensure that they update their 'pen-picture' of a child's needs over time. Reading these scripts suggests this was not always the case.

- *History as context:* assessment of current need is difficult without some understanding of the child's history. There was some variation in the manner in which history was used. Often this was as an appropriate illustration of the underlining cause of need and therefore how that was currently manifest. For instance, from Case 40 *'she will need help to think through what has happened and to help to form a way of coping … the need to be able to express how she feels; the need for people around her to be able to talk openly and to acknowledge that she has this problem … she must have complex feelings for her father, whom she loves, but who murdered her mother.'* Occasionally needs were described purely as narrative, chronicling events in the child's life; such chronology is certainly necessary, but it does not, of itself, offer a sufficient analysis of the child's needs.

- *Generalised or particular descriptions:* how easily can needs be expressed in short phrases, devoid of explanation of the particular circumstances of each case? Where common phrases are used, such as *'security and stability'* or *'to understand who he is and develop self-esteem'*, these can appear to be based on conventional wisdom and on the assumption that such phrases are sufficient without drawing out the particular implications for the individual child. A considered analysis of need requires more than this. This poses a dilemma in searching for word patterns to describe needs. Yes, it is necessary to have a shared conceptual understanding that can be expressed succinctly, but there is a danger that such phrases can become too much of a short hand to be fully explanatory at an individual case level, and develop the characteristics of cliche, and with the potential to replace more considered and individual assessments.

- *Moving away from resource-led definitions:* there are very few instances among the interviews of simple service-led definitions of need; in general, where a need for a service was mentioned this was following a clear exposition of what need that service would serve, for example *'his priority need is for therapeutic work…unless he is able to address issues – regarding his mother, regarding himself, his self-esteem and his feelings – then he is never going to be strong enough to be able to go home.'* However there were many instances where needs were defined in terms of the work to be done but with little specificity as to what that might be – '*there is a need to look at the way the family is functioning; there is work to be done around his self-esteem*'.

- *The needs of the family:* although the primary focus of the social work task – and of these interviews – is the needs of children, often this cannot be separated from the needs of the family. This is especially true in respect of children who are living at home and in receipt of family support services, rather than being looked after.

Descriptions of need: comprehensiveness

The descriptions of need provided in the first unstructured part of the interview were, in general, comprehensive in terms of the range of aspects of a child's life that were covered. On average around twelve different themes or aspects of need were identified for each child.

When each phrase recording an unmet need was considered in terms of the eight developmental dimensions used in the second part of this exercise, this confirmed the comprehensiveness of the range of needs noted by the interviewees. Over 85% of the phrases examined in respect of the 40 cases could be related specifically to one of the eight dimensions; the remainder could not be readily categorised into any of these dimensions. This was often because they were expressed in a general way, or were expressed as needs arising from the child's environment '*His mother had a boyfriend by then and there was a bit of a problem there*'; '*the needs of these children can be individually addressed but by addressing the needs of the sibling groups we stand a better chance of boosting their welfare across the board*'.

Table B.6: *Contents of needs identified in unstructured interviews*

Developmental dimensions		Total	%
1	Protection	45	8.3
2	Health	42	8.0
3	Education	40	7.4
4	Identity	53	9.8
5	Family and social relationships	137	25.4
6	Social presentation	15	2.8
7	Emotional and behavioural development	120	22.3
8	Selfcare skills	10	1.9
	None of these	77	14.0
	Total	539	100.0

Another way of viewing this is at the case level, noting the proportion of cases where a need has been identified relating to the eight developmental dimensions, see Table B.7 below.

Table B.7: *Description of needs, by development areas*

	Protection	Health	Education	Identity	Family/ social r'ship	Social presenta- tion	Emot/ behav devp	Self care skills
Cases in which there is reference	19	18	17	18	32	7	25	5
% of all cases	48	45	43	45	80	17.5	32	15

This shows that two themes were reported in a majority of cases: these concerned family and social relationships and issues relating to aspects of emotional or behavioural development or difficulties. Two themes were only reported in a small proportion of cases: these related to social presentation and selfcare needs – which appear to be related to the age of the child. Between these two ends of the spectrum there were a cluster of descriptive themes that were used in a substantial proportion, just under half, of all cases: these related to health, education, identity and protection issues.

As shall be apparent later, this pattern of needs identified in an unstructured way closely mirrors the pattern of responses to the second, structured part of this exercise, using the *Looking After Children* dimensions of child development.

The comprehensive descriptions of the needs of children offered by the respondents suggests that social workers view the needs of children in a holistic way and they can identify the multiplying effect of a range of needs arising from different areas of the child's life.

The compounding nature of a range of needs is well illustrated by Case 27. This is a three month old baby, K, born prematurely '*so his needs were mainly medical from the outset*'. However, there were also issues around the mother's capacity to respond to the demands of this tiny baby because '*she had quite a marked learning disability and the extended family are also limited intellectually*'. There were also concerns about the mother's capacity beyond his physical needs. '*K needs emotional warmth, there needs to be a promotion of attachment and a secure bond for him*'. Furthermore the mother had been in care as a child and was now living with her parents and was '*looking to those parents who had physically, sexually and emotionally abused her for help to look after the baby*'. The family had an '*expressed need to be able to look after the baby and needed reassurance on that*'. There was no wish on the part of the mother or father for involvement with the baby from the father, but there were genetic issues that could not be ignored so '*regarding his identity K had a need to know his parentage*' and there may be '*medical needs*' arising from his parentage. K is also going to have needs because the '*whole family are firmly rejected by the local community;*' moreover if K is not '*well presented he will suffer the same kind of stigmatisation.*'

The comprehensive nature of the description of needs provided by the respondents is very striking. This must be significant in developing our thinking around the categorisation of children in need. ***The evidence here strongly suggests that when considering the overall needs of any one child that multiplicity of needs may be as influential a measure as the severity of any one particular need.***

This is also likely to have relevance to decisions about the provision of services to children in need. Any scheme for categorising the needs of children must be sufficiently complex to reflect this multiplicity.

Descriptions of need: types of need

There are several ways in which the needs of children were described. First, these reflected the fundamental ***causes*** which give rise to a need – for example, '*the breakup of the family and the rejection by both parents; having been sexually abused, she's extra vulnerable … she's got a need to be protected from vulnerable situations because she is quite vulnerable and naive*'.

Needs were also identified in terms of the way in which they are currently ***manifest***, and which were often described in terms of expressed behaviour; '*she was self-harming, she was liable to cause herself some sort of permanent damage*', which could be followed through in terms of the needs that this expressed behaviour gave rise to – '*kids were trying to bully him … he was retaliating and causing a lot of damage … he had a need for help with anger management*'. Many such descriptions of need can also be seen in terms of ***symptomology***, in that they may be indicative of an underlying developmental problem - *'He has all these needs about his behaviour, but all of these were based on his emotional difficulties, his sense of self ... a very troubled relationship with mother, who had rejected him'*.

Needs were also described in **developmental** terms. Here different time frames may apply, relating to current or future developmental needs. These may be expressed either in terms of a distortion of development from past experiences or as a threat to future development if needs are not met. *'Developmentally there were issues of neglect ... issues of weight loss'*. *'At the moment, because he is only 5, the more extreme elements of his social behaviour are quite charming and funny, but they would be less charming if he was 10 or 12 ... he will need further input to curb some of his aggression and the more extreme elements of his behaviour'*.

Finally, needs may be described in relation to the **current context** or circumstances of the child's living situation, often reflecting the adult carer's ability to respond to the child's needs. *'He lives with a single parent mother who finds it difficult to cope with aspects of his behaviour;'* *'his big need is to be a little boy and he's in a unit that doesn't allow that or in which he gets bullied'*.

In looking at the full range of needs identified for any one child, one would expect to see a balance of these different types of need. None is sufficient on their own to adequately describe the current needs of a child.

This can be illustrated through the example of Case 14, that of a 15 year old boy seen to be at risk of harming himself. The initial contact came from his mother requesting support over his behaviour – staying out, low level criminal activity and possible drug use; further enquiries alleged that the boy was in a sexual relationship with a much older woman, so there was a need for protection from the emotional damage of that relationship and from other possible risks as there was no real certainty about the boy's whereabouts. In describing the boy's needs the social workers identified the cause *'underpinning everything was his relationship with A (older woman) and also with his mum.'* This then leads to an understanding of current needs and how that impacts on several developmental dimensions *'that led to so much instability in his life that it effected every area of need – his physical development, his emotional development, his behavioural development and his social development as well.'* The theme of stability, or lack of it, was identified as becoming manifest in other specific ways. *'He needed sufficient stability to enable him to attend school;'* *The lack of stability in his life put him in a position where he didn't have a GP so there was no regular health monitoring.'*

Descriptions of need: the overall pattern

The pattern of the phrases and words used, in the totality of each of the forty interviews, suggests a range of different emphasis or approaches is being used to analyse need:

- a balance between causes, manifestations and developmental approaches;

- a balance between causal and manifest approaches, including contextual explanation;

- mostly causal and/or contextual explanations of need;

- mostly manifestations, some causal analysis;

- almost all manifestations of need, occasionally linked to service response;

- highly descriptive or anecdotal with very limited analysis of need.

Analysis of the scripts suggests that the first three categories predominate and could be applied in roughly equal proportions to around 70% of the scripts in total. The remaining scripts fell reasonably evenly between the last three categories.

The scripts prompted other descriptive terms which ranged from: very comprehensive to narrowly focused; a thorough knowledge of the child; a very child-centred, in-depth analysis; thoughtful and measured; clear explanatory link between causes, context and current presenting needs; (over) personal interpretation of the child's feelings; conventional or cliched, based on a general understanding of the needs of children rather than this particular child; a few presented long-winded, descriptive accounts.

3 The Developmental Dimensions of Need

The second stage of the interview related to developmental dimensions of need, using the *Looking After Children* (LAC) materials. The LAC materials are now in use in the great majority of social services departments in England and Wales. These materials can be seen in two ways: first they provide a conceptual framework for considering the developmental needs of children in a holistic way; second they are an operational tool to assist social workers in assessing the needs of individual children at different stages of their lives and identifying how any unmet needs could be met. Of course these two purposes will link – the use of the LAC materials as on operational tool is likely to encourage a more holistic, more comprehensive understanding of the needs of children.

Here, the LAC framework was used to explore the way in which social workers perceive and prioritise the different developmental needs of the sample children. An eighth dimension was added to the seven aspects of developmental need included in the LAC materials – this was **significant harm**. Going through each of these dimensions one at a time, respondents were asked to identify any further needs and to prioritise the needs of the child under the eight dimensions as high, medium or low.

Before looking specifically at the results from this exercise there are some general issues arising from the process that are worthy of consideration. These are grouped around the LAC developmental dimensions, the use of the LAC materials and some methodological issues relating to this project.

The Looking After Children dimensions

Several respondents suggested the de-aggregation of some of the dimensions, especially as in this exercise they may wish to prioritise components of a single dimension differently. For example, separating 'health' into 'physical' and 'mental health' (there was also some confusion over mental health and emotional development); splitting 'family and social relationships;' and separating 'emotional' from 'behavioural development'

Almost always these developmental dimensions (LAC + 1) were seen as just that – as dimensions of a child's life or experience which together describe completely the needs of a child; they were only rarely seen as an agenda for considering the ongoing developmental needs of the child.

Regarding the additional dimension 'significant harm', once abuse had been alleged or happened in the past there was then a tendency for this to continue to be seen as a high priority dimension, despite major changes in the child's situation, which may mean that he or she is no longer in immediate risk of significant harm. This reinforces the point made earlier about relating needs to a particular point in time and in relation to whether the child is currently in a safe environment. This is a separate issue from identifying past abuse as an underlying cause of current needs, perhaps through distortion of the developmental process, as discussed earlier.

The use of the Looking After Children materials

Most respondents were familiar with the seven dimensions and had no difficulty in assessing the child's needs under these headings. There were some very clear articulations of the sorts of needs it is appropriate to consider under each heading. For instance, the concept of identity which was understood by the paraphrase – does the child have a sufficiently clear sense of who they are to support the development of self-esteem – brought forth consideration of a range of need whether related to ethnicity, gender, their role in their family, their understanding of their past history.

The relevance of each of the dimensions to every child was occasionally questioned – for example the meaning of selfcare or social presentation needs in respect of a baby?

The exercise of going through each dimension singly and assigning a priority rating separately can discourage any sense of overall prioritisation. Does this point to an inherent tension between addressing needs comprehensively and requiring some sense of focus in order to achieve change?

Methodological issues

There was some inconsistency in the basis on which social workers were asked to consider their priority rating – some indicated it was the priority for their work at that point in time, others saw it in relation to the degree of need the child experienced in a particular area.

It may have been more useful to use a five point rather than a three point priority scale; the scale used did not seem to offer sufficient discrimination to the respondents, for example many wanted to use 'very high', rather than simply 'high'; similarly several implied an intermediate category for instance between medium and high, or medium and low.

4 Developmental Needs: The Priority of each Dimension

This second exercise, focusing on all aspects of the child's development, did not, by and large, bring forth extensive additional areas of need not already mentioned in the free-form first exercise. This reinforces once again the impression of comprehensiveness gained from the first part of the interviews. It did provide an opportunity to be more specific in some areas and to talk about aspects of a child's life that were not presenting problems, where needs were not over and beyond those to be expected of a child of their age. This would suggest that these workers already operate with a concept of needs that is multi-dimensional – perhaps as a result of growing familiarity with the Assessment and Action Records and the understanding upon which they are based.

Table B.8: *The Priority accorded to each developmental dimension*

Dimensions	High		Medium		Low		Totals	
	No %		**No %**		**No %**		**No %**	
Health	14 35.0		16 40.0		10 25.0		40 100.0	
Education	27 67.5		4 10.0		9 22.5		40 100.0	
Identity	26 65.0		9 22.5		5 12.5		40 100.0	
Family & Social Relationships	31 77.5		6 15.0		3 7.5		40 100.0	
Social Presentation	11 28.2		9 23.1		19 48.7		39 100.0	
Emotional /behavioural devp	34 87.2		4 10.2		2 5.1		39 100.0	
Self Care	6 15.4		8 20.5		25 64.1		39 100.0	
Significant harm	21 53.8		7 17.4		11 28.2		39 100.0	

'Emotional and behavioural development' (87% High) and 'family and social relationships' (76% High) stand out as the high priority areas. In contrast 'self care' (64% low) and 'social presentation' (49% low) are seen as less pressing. These priority rating mirror the pattern of frequency in which needs relating to these dimensions were raised in the first exercise. It is possible to reflect on why these particular dimensions are seen as having the greatest priority: do they represent those aspects of a child's life that have the greatest fundamental impact on their wellbeing; do they relate to their undoubted complexity; are these the dimensions of need that present the greatest difficulties for social workers in terms of effecting a positive and lasting change?

There was wide variation in the priority ratings. For example, there were two cases where every dimension was rated highly, and one case with only one high rating. On average respondents scored 4.2 dimensions as high. This overall pattern of priority scoring is likely to reflect the complexity of a case rather than the severity of a particular area of need.

The respondents perceptions of the priority of particular cases did seem to vary by individual. These appeared to be somewhat subjective rather than consistently relating to the extent of needs of the child and how well these were currently being met, judging from the interview scripts as a whole.

This was confirmed by examining the case histories and the interview scripts of five cases which had the highest ratings against those with the lowest ratings. The descriptions of need given in interview would not suggest such a difference in the priority rating. Nor are there many common features among this group of five 'highs' – although all are adolescents, three are disabled children, two with significant impairments that impinge on most aspects of their life, two are looked after and three are living at home.

Similar diversity is apparent in the 'low' group: their ages cover a wider span; three are living at home; one child has severe impairments, but most of his needs are being met leading to this 'low' priority rating; interestingly this group includes two of the children of mixed parentage.

Developmental needs: patterns in descriptions

Some analysis of the text was carried out, using only the second part of the interview – that generated by the responses to the LAC developmental dimensions. As indicated earlier, needs within these dimensions are likely to have already been mentioned in the first part. The purpose was to look for any patterns in the way in which needs were described within these broad dimensions. There are two aspects here: patterns in the actual needs themselves and patterns in the language used to describe needs. Overall the results suggest that because the descriptions of need are closely allied to the particular circumstances of individual children there is as much or more diversity of language as consistent patterns. Details are presented below of some of the patterns in the content of need and in the language used to describe needs within five of the dimensions: namely health, education, social and family relationships, identity and emotional and behavioural development.

Health

Within the descriptions of health needs it is possible to determine eight main themes. These are set out in Table B9 in order of prevalence and with some illustrative examples.

Table B9: *Patterns in health needs*

Content theme	Illustrative Phrase
Specific individual health needs	• an injury to his hand • persistent low level catarrh • Addison's disease • severe hernia
Normal health needs	• medically he was OK • usual health needs of a 14 year-old • her physical health is good
Diet, weight, eating	• a need to watch her weight • he needs to have his diet monitored and be encouraged to eat healthily
Services/medication	• he has a need for medication of caffeine, vitamins, iron and folic acid • because he's premature it's important to give the health visitor access • she has occupational therapy to help her manage her body, her co-ordination better
Living environment – parents, carers	• Mum is not giving her consent to his being immunised • there are a number of health needs not being met at home – she's not had any routine with sleeping and wasn't eating properly
Monitoring	• there needs to be close monitoring by the health visitor • there is a sickle cell trait, so that needs monitoring • she's prone to ear infections, that's got to be kept an eye on because they really do cause her a lot of discomfort
Emotional development	• he needs the therapeutic work to help him deal with his health needs • there is a risk of self harm, that is a health need on one level and emotional development as well

The most common health needs identified were very specific to the individual and therefore had few signs of consistent patterns. The next most common themes were about 'normal' health needs and about weight and diet. Some of the phrases used to describe these needs are listed below to illustrate any patterns in the language employed.

Ways of saying that the child has 'normal' needs:

- he had a medical and medically he was OK;

- he was in good health according to the medical;

- she has the usual health needs of a fourteen and half / fifteen year old;

- her physical health is good and I think she has very low physical health needs;

- L doesn't have any over-riding special needs in terms of health: he's normally fit – he functions perfectly well;

- in terms of physical health, I don't think he has any needs over and above the average child;

- normal things like immunisations, regular health checks, proper dental care, checks for good eyesight;

- a healthy robust child;

- her health needs now are...those of any other similar child;

- I think she has the same health needs as a similar young person;

- he seems to be quite a healthy little child;

- her health needs in herself I think are limited;

- she is a healthy and happy child now;

- he presented as a happy, healthy child who had reached all his developmental milestones because he looked healthy;

- he's a big child, he's a tall child, he's certainly reaching health, height and weight milestones, there's no problems with that;

- any time off school has been genuine flu or something like that;

- he's a healthy boy, so he obviously won't have any health needs;

- she doesn't have any particular health needs;

- she's a normal healthy child;

- he has the health needs of a thirteen year old, of a normal, healthy thirteen year old;

- in terms of his health needs ... they've been fully met;

- I think healthwise he's fine in that he doesn't get illnesses.

Here some patterns of language do emerge notably around the notion of 'normal', 'average', 'for her age' development; and the assumed lack of health needs because a 'child is healthy.'

Ways of describing needs around weight and diet:

- it's the diet again, encouraging him to eat healthily and have exercise because he's such a large boy and that's got to be impacting on his health;

- she has health needs around ... things like healthy diet and the right food to eat;

- she has a weight problem now – she's become quite obese;

- he ate a lot and he was overweight which his mother was concerned about talking about healthy diet ... because he didn't eat that healthily;

- his weight has always been fairly crucial and at one time he was obese;

- C didn't like being overweight but felt that was him: he was a big, fat, ugly, no good, useless, unlucky;

- his weight will always have to be watched;

- maybe weight; I know I discussed with the guardian last week that he looks a bit thin;

- health is important because she is a child who eats an awful lot. Her health needs are really not to be overweight;

- I half wonder whether he's got this sensory atrophy thing where they don't taste anything, they just want to keep on eating, eating, eating to satisfy a need;

- his weight and development generally are monitored very carefully;

- H requires constant supervision, monitoring of protein levels … looking at how often to feed;

- she's a bit overweight really, which I think to watch her weight would be a kind of way of saying it really;

- he'll need to continue eating well and living well;

- he needs to have his diet monitored and he needs to be encouraged and supported to eat healthily.

Although the theme of diet and weight was mentioned a significant number of times there was no consistent pattern in the language used.

Education

Much of the discussion of educational needs revolved around the achievement or development of the child, often a statement of the level of educational attainment standing as an expression of current or future needs.

Similarly the provision of services, or lack of them, was also used as a way of identifying need. The themes that emerged from this section also illustrate the role of education or school in other aspects of a child's life, and visa versa, for instance issues such as relationships and stability. As before, listed below are the main themes expressing educational need and some examples of the phrases used.

Table B10: *Patterns in educational need*

Content theme	Illustrative Phrase
Achievement/development	• she acknowledges that her reading and writing, her literacy skills are quite poor, so that is going to have implications for the care of her children • he is behind in his education • he needs to attend pre-school, here he will be able to develop his social skills and his verbal reasoning
The nature of services	• he needs the water stimulation • he needed a decision to be reached about the fact that he wasn't in school so alternative plans could be made for him to be educated
Living environment	• the parents are very anxious in terms of wanting to know about the statementing process which is some way off • there weren't concerns about her schooling before she came into foster care; once in foster care her behaviour in class went through the ceiling
Relationships	• to enable him to have more appropriate relationships with his peers • he was inclined to be overly aggressive towards other children
Settling/stability	• he found it difficult settling in, in terms of staying within expected boundaries • he needed sufficient stability to enable him to attend school
Absence/attendance/exclusion	• he was out of school completely and this has to be addressed
Future implications	• she's at an important stage in her education, she's got a year of hard work because she does know what she wants out of life now and I think this is the key to it

Ways of describing educational needs that relate to the child's living environment or his parents or carers:

- this boy was under achieving because of the environment in which he was living;

- having his educational needs met.. that's going to be difficult to achieve because he's in a unit where the young people are older and so they don't go to school;

- we're now having to look at financing an independent fostering agency placement until we get something long-term, and the department are now saying that they can't finance both the school and the placement so that is something that's under threat;

- working with the parents and the education department to try and find the most appropriate form of education for him;

- another foster child in the home who's got severe learning difficulties ripped all her school books up and this worried her…;

- this has been a need of hers: for them to understand that it wasn't her fault that did it;

- this learning difficulty that is common amongst all the family members;

- similar issue with K's father, so this is going to be a concern for K;

- the parents are very anxious at this point in terms of wanting to know about the statementing process, which is quite difficult again, because it's some way off;

- the bullying related to also what was going on at home and how the stepfather was with him;

- there were concerns about her school before she came into foster care;

- it's not surprising that he has educational needs, because of his parents.

Studies informing the Framework for the Assessment of Children in Need and their Families

Although there is a common theme to this particular educational need the specific circumstances of each child do not lend themselves to a common use of language.

Identity

Identity was clearly understood as an important developmental need for all children; again, being described in a variety of ways that sometimes relate to context or current situation and sometimes to the way in which needs are currently being met or remain unmet. Examples of the most important themes around identity are set out below.

Table B11: *Patterns of need in respect of identity*

Content theme	Illustrative Phrase
Self perception	• in terms of who she is, where she comes from and why she is where she is • an area of great difficulty because she hasn't really got a very great sense of her own identity at all
Family/carers	• his needs in terms of establishing his identity, need a lot of consideration because his mother's background is so unusual in terms of her life experiences • his identity in terms of his family and the break down of his family and where that placed him was a crucial thing
Need for intervention/services	• he has a life story book which is important to him • I'm trying to talk to her about what roles she has in life, what her role with her mother is – it's all about identity
Withholding/not having information	• he's not expressing much about his birth father… because he doesn't know who his birth father is or very much about him • her (birth father) was not somebody that her other birth family members are happy to discuss with her, so that the whole bit of her life is completely missing
Peer groups/relations	• other kids at school will probably be quite crucial to his sense of identity • he had a peer group that fitted his needs
Self esteem	• because he has such low self esteem and lack of social skills that all impacts on his identity • It's important that he has some sense of self worth and sense of belonging

Table B11: cont.

Content theme	Illustrative Phrase
Ethnicity	• his identity as a black person is quite solid • ethnicity for this particular child was a real difficulty...he actually saw himself as white with blond hair
Difference/alienation	• Addison's disease was very much part of his identity...he was keen to be a pen pal with someone else with the disease, and as a way of not feeling so different • he's never known his father, he's had a couple of step-fathers...he feels there's something wrong with him and that he's different to other young people

Ways of describing needs around the content theme of self-esteem:

- work still needs to be done on his self-esteem;

- because he's got such low self-esteem and lack of social skills so that all impacts on his identity;

- he has got very little sense of self-worth although that is developing now;

- identity needs to be worked on with her: she needs to like herself and I don't think she does at the moment;

- it's important that he has some sense of self-worth and sense of belonging so he's able to – when he grows up – feel comfortable with himself;

- it's very difficult to tell him for D or from D who he feels he is and how much confidence, how much self-esteem that he has;

- she does have identity needs ... all that is happening for her, she doesn't feel she's an OK person, she's ugly, she's fat, she's spotty in her eyes, not in our eyes, she's got no friends, nobody loves her, very low self-esteem;

- his self-esteem is very low: he feels that there's something wrong with him and that he's different to other young people;

- low self-esteem and he views the world as … distorted;

Ways in which the issue of ethnicity was presented:

- his identity as a black person is quite solid;

- so he's able to develop those mechanisms for coping with racism because his mother hasn't been able to do that;

- L needs a family who enables him to build up those defences and helping him cope with racism in later life;

- ethnicity for this particular child was a real difficulty;

- I suppose his ethnic needs from his father's background … there's also the white needs from his mother's background and tying those two together;

- he has needs obviously but I think his needs are met... he has long contact periods with his father, he's lived with a black family where his mother and her partner are black, so his needs are met;

- he's quite comfortable and confident in his black identity. There are black workers at the unit and he has black friends. I think that needs to be ongoing because he's a black child in our country.

These two sets of descriptions of particular themes again suggest that even when the understanding of the need is similar, this is described in a variety of ways.

Family and social relationships

This dimension gave rise to the greatest number of phrases describing need, with over three quarters of these rated as a high priority. Needs around this dimension were most often seen in terms of relations with particular family members or friends; occasionally they were expressed more generally around the child or young person's capacity to make or sustain relationships. Hence one way of arranging the content themes would be in terms of these particular relationships – with mother, with father, with siblings etc. Here themes are selected by the nature of the relationship issue, rather than who the relationship is with; phrases describing need have been placed in only one group, although often they cover more than one theme. The grouping of phrases under this heading are presented in a slightly different way to those in previous sections, with each content theme being illustrated more fully, with longer textual phrases.

Ways of describing the effects of past events or previous unmet needs:

Attachment

- there is a great sort of hollowness to him because he's never had that real security that can only come from real nurturing, unconditional love;

- he hasn't got the things a child needs: a warm, positive relationship with a single, consistent figure;

- there was a gap in that he didn't have any confidence that he was special to somebody, that they would go that little bit further for him because he was special. He didn't seem special to either of his parents.

Proper childhood

- never having had the opportunity to be a child of six, seven or eight, and the mother-daughter relationship that you would hope a child would have at that age;

- she has missed out on a proper childhood of being able to play and having the security and comfort of an appropriate family.

Unknown past events

- this is a high priority for me because of what's happened in the past, and I still need to find out what happened, why it did, and really to get to the truth;

- his emotional development and his behavioural development were really root cause things or root issues. And one that I don't think we ever got to the bottom of. We scratched around the surface.

General

- he was younger when he came into care and he's had such a chequered past that he's not had any needs met;

- he's starting to work out that a lot of what he's experienced is nothing to do with him…the fact that people had abused him, people have rejected him, people have had other priorities like running a school, that they hadn't been able to put his needs first … his behaviour made it difficult in a classroom, because people simply didn't have the time or the facilities to be able to take him to one side and talk him through;

- his behaviour stems from not having his emotional needs met.

Ways of describing the promotion of security:

- K needs emotional warmth, there needs to be a promotion of that attachment and secure bond for him;

- she needs to develop a way of coping emotionally with things she felt;

- but emotionally the thing is for consistence and security;

- the priority for me would have been this whole idea of the lack of stability of care – not in a physical sense: in an emotional sense;

- it's a case where we need to look to the future to try to improve what's happening now to get some kind of stability;

- I think G's needs are to experience security and stability in the family environment, so that during her adolescence she can develop in just the same way as any other child of a young family would be able to do;

- she needs security, she needs emotional security;

- we need to actively promote that and we have been doing so by teaching D about the development of the relationship with her baby, encouraging her to respond to him in an emotional way: touching him, smiling at him, making eye contact – those sort of things that promote the kind of attachment we're looking for. Within that we're trying to promote within D a sense of trying to protect this baby and trying to get her to take responsibility for protecting him and knowing how to do it;

- at the age and stage that he is at now, if he's put into a long-term substitute family, that can be stopped, that cycle can be broken, so it's important, I think, for us to really find this family to stop this escalating, because if it did escalate he would be very very difficult to be placed for adoption;

- he didn't appear to have any significant attachments to any of the adults who were involved with him … and I think he's had that opportunity with his foster carers – to be able to form an attachment to adults that he can trust and learn from that, and so his emotions will develop.

Ways of describing inability to acknowledge, express or deal with feelings:

- I think he would have been happy if we'd all just gone away and left him alone, on one level. But on a more intrinsic, on deeper level, he wanted somebody to make everything ok;

- P had real difficulties empathising … his inability to empathise created real problems…he really, really was unable to do that effectively … and it was much more than just the normal teenage boy inability to empathise;

- it was really hard for him to acknowledge the emotional difficulties that he was having as well – and again you come back to the whole issue of masculinity and how it's portrayed in society, and stuff, but I do think for P it went further than that: I think that he was quite repressed;

- when you asked him about how he felt, what he'd usually reply was he would talk about what was happening to him and not necessarily relate that to how he felt;

Studies informing the Framework for the Assessment of Children in Need and their Families

- he was struggling to deal with all the things that were going off and struggling to come to terms with how he was feeling;

- his mum's history was of being in local authority care … so his mum had experienced lots of rejections, and I don't think it would have been the kind of family that would have generated, or really would have had much experience of people sitting down talking about feeling sad.

Ways of describing reducing risky or inappropriate behaviours:

- he wouldn't stay at school, and I found that really desperately worrying to think of a little boy of nine walking out of school on a really regular basis;

- because it's very difficult with K – with some children you can identify the triggers to difficult behaviour, but with K it's much more complicated than that, so it's very difficult to manage because quite often you can't predict when she's going to, when this behaviour is going to erupt;

- his disability creates behaviour which is deemed inappropriate, so it makes it very difficult to say, 'Does he have emotional, behavioural developmental needs?'

- a problem with him is he's easily led – any naughty boy; he'll run after him, his fine about that, he loves that and he has run off a few times but I actually don't think that's really intentional thing to run away, I think that he's got involved with other children and wandered off with them and wandered outside the area where he's supposed to be, and he'd just literally gets lost;

- she is quite a demanding little girl, and she has a need to behave in a way appropriate to her age. At the moment she behaves like a child in terms of her demands on people;

- my aims were very basic: for R not to harm himself and for us to have some idea of where he was. And to feel confident that where he was somewhere that was safe.

Ways of describing parents' or carers' capacity:

- emotionally his needs were certainly not met, they were quite deprived within that family, but I certainly don't think that it was intentional, I think the parents just did not know what to do with the soiling and wetting;

- the mother's history and her own limitations lead me to suspect that there is less likelihood of them being able to meet K's emotional and behavioural developmental needs;

- the children are the way they are because of the treatment they get from their parents;

- I think he was probably quite emotionally deprived and I think that was because I don't think the parents knew how to cope.

Ways of describing relationships with family:

- her behaviour has become more and more difficult and she seems, because – I think – because of the family instability and all that's happening around her, it's actually becoming quite a major feature;

- a lot of his behaviour came out of him feeling insecure at home with his parents.

Ways of describing self-esteem or unhappiness:

- she sits and listens to all her mother tells me about her, and it's very derogatory…a child labelled by her mother as naughty so she often is;

- he doesn't care about being in school, he doesn't care about himself enough to want to be in school;

- he's a very unhappy, damaged little boy who is probably depressed.

Ways of describing need for boundaries or behaviour management:

- his growing need would be that boundaries would be laid down for him for what he could do and couldn't do, and that can come into the realm of safety as well;

- it's setting up boundaries in the learned behaviours, and it's how he'll be able to use that when he's not in the environment where he's learning it: how he'll be able to take that out into his other life, his family life;

- a high need there to address behaviour within the home which was to be done through working with the parents at regaining control;

- R's inability to accept boundaries escalated, and that was made worse by the fact that the person he claimed was his carer, A, was in fact his partner; and the adult who he claimed was taking responsibility for him – and as part of that responsibility – what I would say, one of those elements of responsibility is setting appropriate boundaries effectively – wasn't actually doing that because she didn't see that as her role, and he didn't see that as her role either, really.

Ways of describing links between emotional wellbeing and behaviour:

- her emotions have led to her bad behaviour;

- I mean, her emotions have led to her bad behaviour, you know, her behaving very badly which led to her being excluded from this family;

- that's just his unhappiness coming out in some bizarre behaviours;

- she's become, sort of, more aggressive recently and I think that's born out of frustration because of her circumstances.

Ways of describing specialist intervention

- at the moment she's got very severe emotional problems … so there's a need for treatment;

- it's uncharted track-territory because these children are so rare that we have to take advice from Manchester on the behavioural side as to what's the best way of handling it and then trying obviously community nurses to try to institute some programme if it's necessary.

Emotional and behavioural development

This dimension also gave rise to many different phrases describing needs. In many instances these recorded the social worker's perception of the child's current state of emotional wellbeing or behavioural difficulties. Often these were linked to their understanding of the underlying causes of any problems; the specific needs related to these symptoms was very often implicit rather than articulated explicitly. Most respondents dealt with emotional and behavioural development separately. Analysis of the descriptions of needs under the emotional/behavioural dimension gave rise to several different content themes. These are shown below with examples of the phrases used by social workers.

Ways of describing stability, security, belonging:

- clearly T is going to need a stable care-giver, but that will not necessarily be his family of course. In order for him to be able to make attachments, so for him to feel emotionally secure;

- she needs a stable family;

- he needs to belong to a long-term family;

- I think he has a very real need to be part of the family;

- her main need is for her grandmother and her need is for real consistency;

- L needs a family who is able to help him build up those defences and helping him cope with racism in later life;

- but the relationship with the mother at the moment is all important to her: it's the one important thing in her life, to get back with this mum and be a part of a family again;

- it's important for L to belong to a family, so he can+ feel wanted, he needs a sense of belonging;

- if we can try and reduce conflict there (in family) then that will create some stability and reduce his anxiety;

- I think that's probably quite a big need really: he needs somehow to feel that it's OK to be happy away from his family.

Ways of describing place within family:

- there were these new families springing up that weren't his and the family that had been his didn't exist;

- these are your parents – you've got good reason to love them – but also they have not always been appropriate carers for you and – you know- it's keeping a balance from one extreme to the other;

- he's angry with them – and understandably he's angry with them – and he is very articulate, he can push them, he can push his father to make him feel guilty, but he sees that it should be his family that's providing for him and not social services, and he tells them that;

- I predict that he (father) may well lose an interest at some stage, if he gets another partner, as I believe will happen. I think he'll increasingly lose interest in being a father to A, perhaps just continue to play a token role in her upbringing. Although they're an argumentative family, D has a place in the family;

- there was stuff about R's relationship with his father and his mother, and his ability to place himself accurately within the context of this family;

- it seemed like everybody else in the family had a particular role apart from P: it was like the oldest child was the oldest child, the second child was the cleverest child, the youngest child was the youngest child. And there was P who was the naughty one;

- the children they are not sure what their role is within the family;

- and the need to be accepted on his terms and perhaps to be recognised as the individual as he is;

- his mum was in a relationship with somebody new, and his dad was also in a relationship with somebody new: both his parents' partners had children who were living with them, and P was not given the same sort of priority in the reconstituted families;

- so it's been quite a big thing for her to be taken away from her home, or to live apart from this family so – And all this pretence of 'I never want to see my mum again: I want to change schools so I don't even have to go near the home' was a facade really because there's a great need for her to be back with her mother.

Ways of describing building and sustaining relationships:

- the only thing I would add is that R's needs in terms of his relationship with his peer group – setting up those kind of things – there were issues that needed to be addressed in some way for R for him to form relationships with young people of the same age;

- and social relationships, again because of her moods that is difficult, it is something that is going to take some considerable time I think to be actually certain about her sexual relationship;

- he knew how far to take it, but he just couldn't, he didn't have those boundaries in most of his communications with others (and that led to quite serious problems for him);

- P's a very, very confrontational young man, very confrontational, and speaks without thinking in a way that creates immense problems for him;

- certainly when he recognises people's voices, he responds to touch or he could play vocal games, where he will try and repeat sounds in the making, not that are formed into words but different sounds, different intonations and different patterns he'll try and copy;

- S's not very good at making and maintaining appropriate friendships with peers;

- once she's out of the care system and after care is reducing, social relationships are all she's going to have to rely on, and I think she's going to find that difficult – she's going to be very isolated;

- when the psychiatrist was with her at the hospital he said that he felt she was, that a lot of her behaviour was coming from social isolation and teachers within the school also said that she'd had problems with peer relationships;

- she did go to school but she was quite alienated from the other children at that point because she was not cared for physically and therefore they backed off her all the time;

- she recognises that people get frustrated with her, people get angry with her. She sees that reaction but doesn't understand the causation really within herself;

- social relationships are going to be hugely important because D's capacity to choose her social relationships with more care is very limited.

Ways of describing rejection, loss:

- (foster placement) turned out to be negative because that placement has broken down – S's probably taken that on board as something that she did wrong within that placement – that was another rejection;

- C can't have the sort of family relationships that he would like – which is to be in the heart of a warm loving family – he can't have that;

- as you know her father died when she was three and recently has been visiting his grave for the first time and I think there's a need still to grieve about that;

- he had been rejected by his birth mother, and two siblings had stayed at home which must have had an emotional effect on him;

- R's relationship with his mother's partner; that was a deeply troubled relationship, and he was very clearly rejecting, rather than rejected by, mother's partner;

- he was actively discouraged from participating in his mum's reconstituted family, and became increasingly discouraged from participating in his dad's reconstituted family. So there were lots of serial rejections for him;

- the family as a whole are firmly reflected by the local community and obviously we would hate to see K suffer the same kind of discrimination that they have.

Ways of describing contact:

- because she lives in the middle of such an awful chaotic family, she has the opportunity to see most members of her family, whether she particularly likes members of her family, but the opportunity is there;

- we need to keep his relationship going with (brother) because he's very fond of (brother) and we need to help him sort that out;

- the other sister who doesn't live at home, we're building contact with her, and she wants contact with him;

- he shows that he doesn't like being away from the family in various ways, and he shows who he enjoys being with and who he doesn't enjoy being with (a disabled child);

- he needs to have his future sorted out really, and he needs to keep contact with his family;

Studies informing the Framework for the Assessment of Children in Need and their Families

- she's got a need to be able to maintain contact and to feel that she's getting something positive from the contact.

Ways of describing roles and models:

- social relationships – it's the peer group: he's not really got an appropriate peer group, that's the biggest thing;

- she doesn't have a model of what a good, well-adjusted family is all about;

- D's (brother) relationships were unsettled, he was in and out of a relationship with a woman much older than himself and because of R's relationship with D and perception of D, I think that had an impact on R's identity;

- I think S has got to the stage where it's too late to do an awful lot about giving her a positive image of family life – she's got her views so set – it would be nice to try and change things, and I think there is a need there;

- I think S's mother has special educational needs and has led quite an unsettled and most unacceptable lifestyle in terms of working as a prostitute – I think S sees that as quite negative because she is that woman's child and that has implications about how S sees herself;

- I think that his mother was quite ashamed that she had had a relationship with somebody from another ethnic background and that the stepfather had terrible needs of his own.

Ways of describing impact of relationships:

- and if he is able to form at least a good, maybe a good marriage, then I think that will – you know it doesn't have to be marriage, but at least a close, warm, fulfilling adult relationship I think would repair so much of the damage that he's experienced in the past;

- I don't want to justify somebody hitting a child – but he has got into disputes with adults who have then hit him. And the way that he communicates...contributes to that whole process;

- the partners of his parents they don't rate as far as S is concerned, so that is always going to be a difficulty, until he can learn to accept his parents' choice of partners;

- it's also important in terms of his sexual offending, because sexual offending can often stem from family dynamics, basically the relationship between a young person and his mother, and his sexual behaviour;

- she's missing having a relationship with her mother – this is why she was so disruptive;

- she therefore subjects K to being part of her own social network which is sometimes not as helpful as we would like.

Ways of describing self-esteem:

- C is very shy and I think because his self worth is so low, he'll often present as aggressive and has been absolutely foul-mouthed in the past: his language at one time was depraved – there's no other word for it – particularly if he felt he'd been hurt by people;

- because that's where his whole source of comfort and identity and things like his self-identity will come from his social relationships;

- he's not very good with his peer group, so he could do with some help around that, but until he starts to feel better about himself he's not likely to be able to improve being able to get on with other children;

- for work within peer relationships – yes it's about assertiveness and she struggled with asserting how she felt about things. I did do a bit of work with her on assertiveness;

- because it will all be part of her identity and her competency as a person to be able to form social relationships.

Ways of describing need for knowledge or information:

- wants to know about his father and he never talks about grandparents or uncle or any cousins, and not everybody knows about them, and I guess I've been drawn into the secret because I don't talk about them as well;

- I think it's important for him to know about his extended family;

- for him it's I need to know about my father but I'm also quite frightened of him;

Ways of describing conflictual families:

- his family had broken down and the level of dispute between his parents was immense…and he was very easily able to play one off against the other;

- the difficulty arises with the relationship between A and B and F and B, which in the future will pose more difficulties as time goes on;

- needs to have help with his relationship with his brother because the boys have a very conflictual jealous relationship.

Ways of describing need to improve family functioning:

- there was a need to change the parenting roles and bring the parents into a more consistent way of parenting;

- there was a huge need to change the way the parents were reacting, or treating C, and giving her more space so that she could therefore respond to them differently;

- there was a need to work at that relationship, that family relationship, to change the way that the family was functioning.

Ways of describing need for distance, protection:

- he needs contact with (family)…but he can't because it's not appropriate and it wouldn't be safe because his family would encourage him to run off;

- the need for contact with the rest of birth family – it's not crucial but in an ideal world it would probably be better for him if he was with C for instance, it's not safe because she's taught him and encouraged him to run;

- he also has a need to feel protected and safe;

- I don't think he would develop to his full potential because of the hazards that mum brings with her: because of the dysfunctionalness that mum brings with her, it wouldn't be good for L.

Studies informing the Framework for the Assessment of Children in Need and their Families

5 The Causes of Need

The final exercise was to ask social workers to indicate which of a given list of seven 'causes of need' were applicable to each child, and to choose from this the main cause of need. This was expressed by asking social workers to consider whether 'this child is in need as a result of …'. Regarding the process, few respondents experienced any difficulty in readily identifying one or more cause of need and the main cause of need. Once again before presenting the results, some general points about the exercise are worth noting.

- no-one chose the option 'none' as a response; this suggests that these categories reflect the workers' own framework for considering the causes of need;

- two people suggested a further – similar -category; 'a child in need as a result of being in care.' One related to the fact that the care system had not come up with an appropriate placement which had resulted in a further increase in the needs of the child; and the other related to the general stigma and loss of esteem likely to be felt by a young person in public care;

- most found it relatively easy to choose a 'main' category; in three instances joint main categories were given (but they were encouraged to consider this by the questioner);

- the discussion by the respondents as they made their allocations highlights the importance of each of the different elements included in these descriptions. For example, respondents articulated the difference between 'rejections from', or 'estrangement from', or 'collapse of a family'. To offer abbreviated versions of these categories may well reduce their relevance and validity;

- judging by the speed of response in allocating to categories, this exercise did not appear to pose too many problems, increasing confidence in the usefulness of this analytical framework.

The distinction between the different approaches to need used in this study was grasped by the interviewees without any difficulty. The scripts suggest that most respondents were very clear about the concept the 'causes of need' and saw this as relating to root causes rather than simply something that was a present factor. They readily moved from one way of describing need to another. Although carried out fairly rapidly there were some clear and thoughtful articulations given for the choice of main cause of need. *There were some issues about the physical chastisement … it was never seen as significant harm…also other dangers about medication and being left alone … that wasn't the root of what was going on, that was the effect of what was going on, so no, the child is not in need as a result of abuse'.*

Despite the apparent ease with which respondents were able to allocate a case to a group, taking the interviews as a whole one gets an impression of descriptions of need that are case specific, and appropriately so. Any conceptual underpinning seems to be an understanding of the needs of all children and from that of each particular child; there is no strong sense that the needs of these children arise because they fall into a particular group as in the above classification.

Causes of need: categorisation

The results from this exercise are presented in Table 12. Note that 'main type' has 45 responses because 'joint equal' responses were recorded for a small number of cases.

The results of this exercise can be compared to that undertaken previously and re-produced in Table 13. Because of differences in the sampling and methods employed in these two exercises, these comparisons should be treated with some caution.

Once again, the importance of multiple causes of need is demonstrated with 3.5 categories, on average, being noted as applicable to a case; an even higher figure than previously.

Table B.12: *Causes of need*

Children in need as result of:	Any mention N	%	Main Type N	%
1. Physical condition, disability or development difficulties	19	47.5	6	13.3
2. Deprivation, poverty or social disadvantage	11	27.5	0	0
3. Parent or carers' disability, illness or addictions	14	35.0	5	11.1
4. Abuse or (wilful) neglect	27	67.5	6	13.3
5. Living in unstable or otherwise detrimental family	33	82.5	18	40.0
6. Breaking the law	8	20.0	1	2.2
7. Rejection from, estrangement from or collapse of family	26	65.0	9	20.0
8. Other reason	2	5.0	0	0.0

Table B.13: *The causes of need as presented in the Mori/York/NCB study*

Children in need as result of:	Any mention N	%	Main Type N	%
1. Physical condition, disability or development difficulties	145	32.3	56	13.9
2. Deprivation, poverty or social disadvantage	182	40.3	16	4.0
3. Parent or carers' disability, illness or addictions	172	38.3	65	16.1
4. Abuse or (wilful) neglect	154	34.3	59	14.6
5. Living in unstable or otherwise detrimental family	263	58.6	77	19.1
6. Breaking the law	97	21.6	58	14.4
7. Rejection from, estrangement from or collapse of family	168	37.4	57	14.1
8. Other reason	22	4.9	15	3.7

This exercise has produced less clustering of responses. The most common contributory factor – 'living in unstable or otherwise detrimental family' was identified in more than eight out of ten cases; although this was also the most common factor in the earlier exercise, it was reflected in fewer than six out of ten cases.

This greater diversity is also apparent in the main causes of need. Here this ranged from no-one identifying poverty as a main cause to 40% of respondents selecting the 'unstable family' as a main cause. In the previous exercise responses were more evenly spread across all reasons with the most commonly identified main cause – also 'unstable family' – being applied to less than 20% of cases.

Also noticeable is the very low number of cases – 2.2% – where 'breaking the law' was identified as a main cause; this compares to a figure of 14.4% from the first study.

There is also discrepancy in the two sets of results in the ordering of the main causes of need, although significantly the top and the bottom causes are the same, namely 'unstable family' as most important and 'breaking the law' as least important.

The social workers participating in this exercise found these categories for describing the causes of need in children as meaningful and relevant. This would suggest the categories have some value. Yet on the two occasions when they have been used they have produced results that have varied somewhat. This is likely to reflect the different composition of the sample and the different methods used to gather the information.

This exercise seems to confirm the value of this categorisation of causes of need; the actual distribution of cases within that categorisation needs to be tested further, before the result can be treated with confidence.

Studies informing the Framework for the Assessment of Children in Need and their Families

6 *Concluding Remarks*

The main aim of this exercise was to inform our thinking about the way in which the needs of children can be described and to test again possible mechanisms for doing so. As noted in the Introduction, interest in describing the needs of children flows from two concerns: to enhance standards in assessment of needs through the development of appropriate tools which focus primarily at case level; at a system level to consider whether it is possible to develop a framework to categorise children in need into distinctive groups through aggregation of information on individual children and their needs. The former encourages an approach to describing need that is comprehensive and expansive; the later one that seeks to synthesise and simplify.

These represent two very different end purposes. This project aimed to test the feasibility of serving both purposes using the same data. It would seem that this is possible, so long as there is clarity about how the analysis of data is to be used. In assessing need in individual cases identifying all areas of need is essential. In understanding a total child population simplification and categorisation in a meaningful way is necessary. This is well understood. The real issue is developing frameworks that allow both uses to be appropriately served from the same information source, gathered in a consistent and efficient way.

There were three parts to the original interviews: a free flowing description of the child's needs; a description of need using the LAC dimensions; a classification of the causes of need using the Mori\York\NCB formulation. Although this project has produced 'findings', the main interest lies in our greater understanding of the process of describing the needs of children. Some very general conclusions from this exercise are summarised below:

The descriptions of need given in the free-flowing exercise were, for the most part, closely allied to pertinent factors or situations facing or likely to face the child and then to the needs arising from this. These descriptions were only rarely narrative descriptions of events or a view of needs that was resource-led, apart from those instances of 'the need to look at ...' or 'the need to work on...' . While the descriptions overall covered similar content areas, they were largely case specific. Neither were they over- characterised by jargon or cliche. They did not therefore present ready patterns in their phraseology.

The descriptions were comprehensive and multi-faceted. Taken as a case-package they combined descriptions that reflected causes of need, manifestations of need arising from current presenting problems, needs relating to the child's overall development and needs deriving from the context in which the child was living.

The nature of the first exercise encouraged expansive descriptions of need; with no consistent invitation to identify a priority need. This mitigated against using the results to identify clusters of need.

Using the LAC developmental dimensions (plus an additional one on protection) as a second framework for describing need did not draw out substantially more areas of need, confirming the breadth of the early descriptions. The interviews also demonstrated a ready recognition of the dimensions by respondents, suggesting that these developmental dimensions have been internalised by many practitioners. The developmental dimensions were seen most often as aspects of a child's life to be included in assessment, rather than restricting this to unmet need or needs unlikely to be met in the future. Hence many of the identified 'needs' were currently being met or appropriate arrangements were in place.

In prioritising these aspects of need, 'family and social relationships' and 'emotional and behaviour development' stand out as the area of need referred to most often in exercise one and as the highest priority in exercise two (although inconsistency in questioning suggest caution in interpreting this result too specifically).

Analysis of the descriptions offered under these headings suggest some patterns to the content of needs, but only limited consistency in the language used to describe these.

The third exercise, to determine which of a choice of 'causes of need' were applicable to each case, presented few difficulties for respondents. The categories offered appeared relevant and meaningful. Again several 'causes' were seen to apply to each case, but most respondents selected a main cause with relative ease.

Taken together all three of these exercises highlight the multiplicity, the complexity, and the compounding nature of the needs of the these children. This suggests that when considering the needs of any one child that the multiplicity of needs may be as important as the severity of need in respect to a single aspect. It also suggests that to make sense of children in need we have to understand how those multiple needs cluster into meaningful groups.

Appendix 1

The Categorisation of Children in Need

The third part of this exercise was to test again the categorisation of the causes of need used as part of earlier study. The focus of this earlier study, commissioned by the Department of Health and undertaken by a consortium of MORI, University of York and the National Children's Bureau, was to examine the formula used to determine the Children's Standard Spending Assessment. A necessary first step in the study was to identify children in need who were known to social services departments. This turned out to be more complex than anticipated. First, the results of a survey of the definitions of 'children in need' used by local authorities produced over 100 different ways of describing children in need. Second, the descriptions of children in need as defined by the planners were not used at a case level to classify cases according to the nature of the identified needs.

If social services are to plan effectively to meet the needs of children they need a framework for describing and categorising these needs. That means making sense of the over 100 different descriptions of children in need used in local authorities.

In examining the descriptions of children in need provided by the survey of SSDs it is clear that they relate to different dimensions. Some relate to the *fundamental cause of need* in children – such as 'child with physical, learning or sensory disabilities' or 'children whose parents have a mental health problem.' Some are an expression of how these **needs become** *manifest* – 'at risk of being accommodated because of family difficulties' or 'committing criminal offences.' Others refer to the *local authorities responsibility or response* – such as 'young person leaving care' or 'child in private foster arrangement'.

Several ways of grouping the descriptions of need were formulated; the one which was best able to encompass most of the 100+ descriptions was a categorisation based on causation or aetiology of need. This gave rise to seven underlying causes for a child being in need. These are:

- *Child in Need as a result of their own physical condition, disability or developmental difficulties;*

- *Child in Need as a result of deprivation, poverty or social disadvantage;*

- *Child in Need as a result of parents'/carers' disability, illness or addictions;*

- *Child in Need (of Protection) as a result of abuse or (wilful) neglect;*

- *Child in Need as a result of living within unstable, stressed, conflictual, emotionally or developmentally damaging family;*

- *Child in Need as a result of breaking the law;*

- *Child in Need as a result of rejection from, estrangement from, or collapse of their own family.*

The opportunity arose within the original study to test this categorisation in telephone interviews with social workers in respect of approximately 450 children for whom they were responsible.

Social workers were asked to identify which of the causes of need apply best to each child, allowing them to identify more than one cause. If they thought none of these categories were appropriate they could give 'none of these' as a response. Next, the social worker was asked, if more than one cause has been identified, was the main cause of need. The results from this exercise are shown below.

Children in need as result of:	Any mention N	%	Main Type N	%
1. Physical condition, disability or development difficulties	145	32.3	56	13.9
2. Deprivation, poverty or social disadvantage	182	40.3	16	4.0
3. Parent or carers' disability, illness or addictions	172	38.3	65	16.1
4. Abuse or (wilful) neglect	154	34.3	59	14.6
5. Living in unstable or otherwise detrimental family	263	58.6	77	19.1
6. Breaking the law	97	21.6	58	14.4
7. Rejection from, estrangement from or collapse of family	168	37.4	57	14.1
8. Other reason	22	4.9	15	3.7

Two observations on this data are relevant here: first, the small proportion of respondents (3.7 per cent) who saw the child's need arising from a cause other than one of the seven substantive options offered suggests this list has potential as a workable tool; second, the needs of these children are multi-faceted with an average of three options being recorded for each child.

This study was also able to relate information on the services received by these children to their 'causes of need.'

Further details of the findings from this exercise are reported in *Categorisation of children in need*, by Ruth Sinclair and Roy Carr-Hill (1997) and available from John Rowlands, Department of Health, Wellington House 135-155 Waterloo Road, London SE1 8UG.

Language of Children in Need: Outline for Interview Schedule

Exercise 1

How would you describe X's needs?

What other needs does he/she have?

You have given me a number of needs, which would you regard as having the highest priority?

How did you go about assessing X's needs?

Exercise 2

*Looking at X's needs in relation to each of the dimensions of the Looking after Children Assessing Outcomes (and the additional dimension we have added in relation to need for protection) can you indicate whether you would **give high, medium or low priority** to ensuring that each need is met?*

What **health** needs does X have?   High   Medium   Low

What needs does X have in relation to
his/her **education**?   High   Medium   Low

What needs does X have in relation to
his/her **identity**?   High   Medium   Low

What needs does X have in relation to
his/her **family and social relationships**?   High   Medium   Low

What needs does X have in relation to
his/her **social presentation**?   High   Medium   Low

What needs does X have in relation to
his/her **emotional and behavioural
development**?   High   Medium   Low

What needs does X have in relation to
self-care skills?   High   Medium   Low

Significant harm: what needs does X have
in relation to **protection**?   High   Medium   Low

Exercise 3

Using a third approach to describing need I am going to read out a list of categories or descriptions of causes of need and I would like you to tell me which descriptions apply to X and identify the main cause.

	a cause	main cause
This child is in need as a result of their own physical condition, disability or developmental difficulty.	❏	❏
This child is in need as a result of deprivation, poverty or social disadvantage.	❏	❏
This child is in need as a result of parents'/carers' disability, illness or addiction.	❏	❏
This child is in need (of Protection) as a result of abuse or neglect.	❏	❏
This child is in need as a result of living in an unstable, stressed, conflictual, emotionally or developmentally damaging family.	❏	❏
This child is in need as a result of breaking the law.	❏	❏
This child is in need as a result of rejection from, estrangement from, or collapse of their own family.	❏	❏
This child is in need as a result of none of these categories. *(please specify)*		

Study C

Assessment in child protection and family support: report of an SSI study

Diana Robbins

Study C: Contents

1 Introduction

This report summarises the findings of a study of assessment in family support and child protection which was completed by a group of Social Services Inspectors (SSI) during the first half of 1998. The aims of the study were:

- **to investigate the process of assessment by social workers in a range of contexts – selected Social Services Departments (SSDs), voluntary organisations and health settings;**

- **to reflect useful lessons from all sectors back to the field;**

- **to look particularly at *innovative* elements in assessment, in all sectors; and**

- **to inform the development of the new framework for assessing children and families (Department of Health et al, 2000).**

The names of the Inspectors involved in the study appear in Appendix 1 at the end of the report. The methods they used to collect data included semi-structured interviews with managers and key workers and analysis of documents, including policy documents and guidance on procedures as well as reporting instruments and case files. In some places, Inspectors were able to observe the assessment process at first hand; in some others, it was possible to interview parents involved in the process. They set out to establish in detail, for each setting:

- who performs what function in relation to assessment, and in what way;

- how information is generated, analysed and used as a basis for providing services;

- what policies, procedures and practices are in place; and

- how all of these impact on individual cases.

- A fuller account of the methodology used in the study appears in Appendix 2.

In all, eleven sites were studied over a three month period. These covered 4 SSDs where new and interesting approaches to assessment procedures were being developed: one research project being undertaken by a team from the University of Leicester School of Social Work on behalf of North Lincolnshire Home-Start in partnership with North Lincolnshire Children's Joint Planning Locality Group (a multi-agency group with representatives from social services, health, education, housing and the voluntary sector). Two large specialist units, and four smaller units run by voluntary organizations. Inspectors were very grateful for the time and effort which managers and staff committed to co-operating in the study, and for the interest they showed in sharing their ideas. The names and addresses of the sites are included in Appendix 3: where individual sites are named in the text, they will be identified by the name and number given in the Appendix.

This was in no sense an "inspection" of the sites. Inspectors had been alerted by contacts with the field to the existence of new approaches, and the purpose of their visits was to explore, analyse and report on them as a contribution to the development of the debate about current practice in this field.

2 *The Study*

The purpose of the study can be simply stated. Some localities or agencies have the reputation for innovative practice in the area of assessment. The study targeted these in order to establish in what ways they represent innovation in practice, and why. What is the practice based on; from what does it derive? What are the links between the nature of the agency, its philosophy, policies and procedures, and good outcomes for children and families? In effect, Inspectors were hoping by the use of detailed instruments, interviews, observation and documentary analysis to deconstruct examples of innovative practice, learn from what has gone well or badly, and offer lessons about their component parts to be copied or adapted into the practice of other agencies.

Although the aims may have been straightforward, putting them into operation inevitably raised difficult questions about the nature of evidence. What does "good" mean in this context? In whose opinion? At no time in the study has an Inspector been able to pursue a case through systematically collected records to the point where it would be possible to say that a particular intervention had been proved to be effective in the long term. Evidence about outcomes was generally rather thin on the ground. But there are examples of reported effectiveness; and Inspectors have been able, by sifting the range of opinions expressed on site, through the documentary evidence, and through their own knowledge and experience, to identify *situations and processes likely to contribute to successful outcomes*. The issue of "cost–effectiveness" has also been raised in the field-work, but cost data, which would enable a judgement to be made about relative cost-effectiveness of different approaches and different settings, has rarely been available.

"Innovation" has also proved to be another slippery term. There were some clear examples of innovatory practice among the sample, where holistic approaches to assessment were being translated into useable forms and procedures. There were also some refreshing examples of systems in which detailed consideration of race and culture was genuinely informing the assessment in ways which could be used positively in the future. Many of the specific techniques and disciplines which were brought to bear on the assessment process proved to be familiar – perhaps deployed in new combinations. But some of these new combinations were themselves of interest, and will be reported in the pages which follow. Developments in specialist units, while not perhaps exactly "innovative", are certainly important elements in the assessment scene; and their ways of working may hold useful lessons for practice in wider settings. Similarly, several SSDs are pioneering technical improvements to recording which deserve wider dissemination.

Establishing a causal connection between a particular intervention and eventual outcome is notoriously difficult. In this study, Inspectors have been looking at four different dimensions of "connection":

- the vertical connection between senior management statements and intentions, and practice on the ground; for the purposes of this study, we can call this
  FOLLOW-THROUGH

- the parallel, vertical connections between levels of policy-making – philosophy, theory, policy, strategy, procedure;
  CONGRUENCE

- the horizontal connections between agencies, at every level of policy and practice;
  JOINT WORKING

- and the connections between all of these and the views of users and carers;
  PARTNERSHIP.

To what extent do these connections exist in sites advertised as examples of innovation in good practice, and how do they contribute to the final result?

One important way in which these links may be maintained is through the documents routinely used in assessment for guiding practice and recording work. Early on in the study, Inspectors identified eight factors which militated in favour of procedural documents effectively implementing policy.

Are procedures:

- owned, through local sometimes informal development of policy and procedures;

- known, through training and experience;

- available – are copies to hand?

- accessible – clearly structured and of usable length;

- clear and specific - plain English;

- demonstrating consensus – commonly understood and agreed definitions;

- current – updated and alive;

- consistent – do the records accurately reflect practice?

Documentary evidence from site visits about procedures was reviewed in the light of these criteria.

For each SSD or unit, some aspect of the work being done was thought to be of especial interest, which justified the choice of site. The remainder of this report will be concerned with what Inspectors found during the visits, and the reflections on assessment generally stimulated by the practice they observed and analysed.

3 *Assessment*

"Treatment itself is intimately bound up with assessment, relying on it as a house relies on its foundation. Consequently, assessment continues throughout the treatment process, despite a change in focus during its course." (Jones, 1997).

The term "assessment" will be used throughout this report to describe a range of situations in which practitioners are attempting in a structured way to arrive at judgements about the nature and severity of the problems confronting children and families which come to their attention, in order to propose solutions. The practitioners include medical and social work staff, psychiatrists and psychologists and, on occasion, education professionals. They will be trying to assess "need" – requiring a response such as treatment, services and/or support – and they will often be trying to assess "risk of significant harm", to the child of staying in the current situation. The sophistication of these assessments can and should relate to different purposes; but not all assessments at the same apparent "level" have the same purpose. A "screening" assessment, for example may be undertaken to see whether there is any need at all; to determine whether the child and family is suitable for the kind of assessment/therapy on offer; to begin the process of collecting basic information; or to identify immediate needs which should be responded to urgently, without the kind of delay which undertaking a fuller assessment can involve.

Each agency may identify the levels and purpose of each level differently. In any context involving actual or probable harm to the child, assessment of the nature of that harm and how to protect the child in the immediate and long-term must take precedence over every other kind of judgement. And how these assessments are seen will of course relate both to the action which follows assessment; and the extent to which the local assessment system is found to be "successful". A wide range of interpretations, systems and approaches is covered by the sample of sites visited by Inspectors. At one end of the spectrum, very straightforward assessments as a basis for low-level family support were offered by one small unit; at the other, intensive, highly professional and complex work was being undertaken with families with multiple problems. In some cases, assessment was seen as a one-off, time-limited activity; in others, the process was described as one of continuing re-assessment. In Kingston, for example, the process was described as **ongoing and integral** to other activities.

Terminology varied widely from site to site. For the purposes of the study, Inspectors identified three basic types of assessment in work with children and families:

- preliminary screening, to establish basic data, supply immediate or urgent services/ protection/ support, refer on or take no further action;

- an initial assessment, to establish more detail about the history, situation and needs of the child, and the family;

- a comprehensive assessment, to develop a full picture of the risks of significant harm, challenges, capacities and needs of both children and families, as a basis for planning future treatment and support.

At each site, the kinds of *assessments routinely undertaken* were established against the background of this typology, as well as the kinds of *assessment involved in the cases which were reviewed*. In the summary which follows, the terminology used at the site will be shown in bold. It does not necessarily coincide with the Inspectors' tripartite division, shown above. More detail about the assessment procedures being developed at the time of the study in some SSDs will be found in Chapter 7: again, their terminology will be followed.

Types of assessment at each site:

1 Kingston SSD
Procedures and guidance allowed for a range of different levels and types of assessment (see Chapter 7). The cases studied covered:

> *Case (a)*
> a **safeguarding** assessment, triggered by evidence of injury to the child, and a **child in need** assessment; appointment of a key worker,

and disclosure of sexual abuse are followed by a **S47 "planning meeting"**, the initiation of care proceedings, and a **comprehensive** assessment of the family, in a residential family centre;

Case (b)

an **initial** assessment, followed by a **child in need** assessment – again, involving the whole family at a family centre;

Case (c)

an **initial** assessment, to establish the needs of an "unsafe", aggressive child and his mother.

2   Stockport SSD

Stockport's procedures allowed for three stages: referral and recording of basic information **(screening)**, **Initial** and **Core** assessments. No cases assessed under these then new procedures were available.

3   Westwood House, Peterborough Family Care, Northampton

Most assessments undertaken by this unit were residential and **comprehensive**, and usually related to Court proceedings. Day assessments were also undertaken. All three cases studied involved child protection issues.

4   North Lincolnshire SSD (Children's Joint Planning Locality Group/Home-Start North Lincolnshire/University of Leicester)

The purpose of the study was to develop a Child and Family Assessment tool which could be used by professionals from a range of agencies to identify "good enough parenting". This would serve as a combined screening *and* initial assessment, which could then be referred on to relevant agencies for further assessment or other action.

5   Nottinghamshire SSD

The Assessment, Planning, Implementation and Review (APIR) system of recording assessments used by Assessment and Reception Teams in this Department provided frameworks for two levels: **Level One screening** and **Level Two initial** assessments. If the need for a **comprehensive** assessment was identified at initial level, an "Orange Book" assessment will be undertaken (Department of Health, 1988). Cases involving each of these levels were studied.

6   Woodside Assessment Centre (NSPCC), Birmingham

Assessments at this centre were described as **comprehensive** child and family assessments, carried out either in person or "on paper". Both kinds were represented in the cases studied by Inspectors: two cases specifically related to child protection, and the third to the making of a residence order although there had been child protection concerns in this case in the past.

7   Bewick Family Centre, Gateshead

Again, only **comprehensive** assessments were carried out at this Centre, sometimes described as "Orange Book" assessments. The cases seen involved firstly, child protection, and secondly, reunification.

8   Park Hospital, Oxford

A range of assessment and treatment options were available at the Unit, including **initial** and **comprehensive** assessments. The three cases covered by the study were:

> *Case (a)*
> an **initial "child in need"** assessment;

> *Case (b)*
> a **comprehensive, day assessment**, where there were child protection concerns;

> *Case (c)*
> a longer-term, **comprehensive residential assessment** dealing with child protection and reunification.

9   Marlborough Unit, London

The Unit offered a range of services, including **comprehensive** family assessments. Three of the latter were studied: two involved current care proceedings; the third – parental responsibility and residence issues, although there had been child protection concerns in this case in the past.

10   Broxtowe Family Centre

The Centre offered initial assessments, particularly focusing on family support.

11 Kensington and Chelsea SSD

The SSD's assessment process consisted of referral plus recording of basic information **(screening)**, followed by a needs assessment. Staff could move sideways to parallel child protection procedures at any stage where risk of significant harm became the major concern. An earlier pilot project found a three stage assessment process to be too cumbersome in practice.

Terminology which is clear to the social workers using it is obviously very important – the APIR framework, for example, was welcomed by staff precisely because it made clear the distinctions and transitions between levels. But it is also difficult: a simple sequence of "levels" may not apply to the complexities of an individual case, and the situation is further complicated when more than one agency is involved. A case may suddenly move "sideways" into child protection procedures. Inspectors found that systems which were backed up by clear guidance about how they were to be used, and – above all – how higher or different levels were "triggered", were most useful to staff. The very complexity of the situations in which staff were working with made the process of developing, understanding and owning local procedures potentially very useful.

There was also considerable variation between sites in respect of the *contexts* in which assessments were undertaken. Inspectors tried to assess the "welcome" which families would encounter at their first referral to a given setting. The variety of ways in which referrals were made meant that only a few reception areas were seen in the course of the study: they were typically rather bleak and formal. But facilities for undertaking assessments were more encouraging. SSDs were doing some assessment work in the office, but also – frequently – in the family home. They were also increasingly making use of family centres for joint work on assessing children and families. The specialist units, in general, used a combination of visits to the home; periods of residential assessment; and trips to shops or other potentially stressful settings in order to monitor parent/child interaction. Only one of the centres – the Woodside Assessment Centre – provided no "on site" assessments: two workers saw families either in their own homes, or in other appropriate community facilities. Residential facilities varied from adequate to good; and facilities for observation (such as one-way screens) and therapeutic work were generally good.

4 Innovation

This study was specifically concerned with innovation – not because something new is necessarily essential to good practice, but in order to bring the most complete, up-to-date thinking to bear on the Departmental review of assessment, and to share it with the field. Innovation may imply *novelty:* actions which have not ever been attempted before, or in quite this way; something genuinely new, or perhaps a combination of familiar parts producing a new whole. It may also mean testing something known to be effective in one context in a *new one*.

Much that was seen by Inspectors was familiar, but **innovation was found** in the senses described above in three different contexts:

- in the context of developments which more clearly linked theory to practice at the "hard end" of assessment (see Chapter 6). These were found particularly, but not exclusively in the more sophisticated specialist units;

- in new kinds of procedures being developed by some SSDs in an attempt to accommodate revised, holistic or preventive goals for practice. Some of these will be considered in more detail in Chapter 7; and

- in the use to which specialist units were increasingly being put, by the Courts and by SSDs (Chapter 8).

Another important meaning of innovation relates to the **innovative capacity** of individual agencies. A commitment to the systematic review of practice, and a culture of flexibility which welcomes development was in several sites found to contribute to good practice.

At the Woodside Assessment Centre in Birmingham, a small team shares a clear purpose and identity, and combines a commitment to open communication with a commitment to reflective practice. They attribute the good level of practice they achieve partly to the clear management and supervision framework within which they work.

In the Park Hospital Unit in Oxford time is set aside for reflection and review every Friday, and this review is carried out within a context of mutual, professional respect and support.

The new procedures introduced by Kingston SSD have contributed to the development of thoughtful practice, and represent a balance between prescription and reflection/flexibility. This is in contrast to the situation found at another site where the implementation of a new system had produced limited effects on the quality of work. In the second case, disappointing results were identified by Inspectors with lack of time for reflection and the absence of a culture which supported creativity and innovation.

This willingness to promote and accommodate innovation has sometimes been identified with the medical model in which practice may be constantly reassessed in the light of new evidence. Certainly, it was found by Inspectors in those specialist units which were led by graduates of this tradition.[1] But there is another tradition which is equally relevant: the development of evaluation of social policy, and so-called "self-evaluation" as a tool of project management. The techniques which have been tested by both statutory and voluntary agencies as a means of promoting effective and responsive action to achieve clearly articulated goals could be part of every plan to implement new procedures for assessment, and were found both in SSD and specialist settings.

---

[1] Both elements – reflection, and a capacity for change in the context of mutual respect – are described in the account of the whole day assessments carried out at the Child and Family Psychiatry Unit in Gateshead in WHEELER John, BONE David and SMITH Jill (1998): "Whole-Day Assessments: a Team Approach to Complex Multi-Problem Families", Clinical Child Psychology and Psychiatry, 3(2):169-181.

5 *Theory and Practice*

In every setting, Inspectors asked about the theoretical perspectives which people working with the assessment process brought to bear on their work. The majority of responses to this question are summarised below. But in some areas, they encountered considerable confusion about what theory was. Some respondents talked about "dignity" and empowerment as their theoretical base: others referred to legislation or guidance as providing it. There were some instances of individuals listing a number of theoretical authorities, but providing no evidence as to how these names linked to what they actually did.

These examples argue, firstly, for **clarity** about the different influences on local practice. Confident and effective practice depends on workers being able to distinguish between:

- the values which they and their agency support, combined in the philosophy which underpins their practice;

- the theoretical framework set by their agency and/or their professional background; and

- the demands of legislation and guidance (which in turn will reflect values and theory).

Secondly, the relevance of theory to effective practice could have been clearer to some respondents, with obvious implications for training. At one site, workers expressed their need for "refresher" training in the context of new procedures; and training was an important theme at sites which showed theoretical clarity and coherence.

Some managers and workers in SSDs replied that they were "theoretical pragmatists", bringing a "bit of this and a bit of that" to bear on the dilemmas they faced. Some of these replies were unnecessarily rueful. Seden's (1999) Review of Literature (see Study A) comments that an eclectic approach to theory may be entirely appropriate to the social work task. Flexibility in the face of complex, varied and changing situations may in fact be promoted by the kind of training social work students receive in a range of theories. It may also be inevitable in terms of the whole agency, since managers will have to depend to some extent on the differing theoretical backgrounds which new recruits bring to the team. However, none of this is the same as saying that "trial and error" – reported as the theoretical perspective of one respondent – is a coherent or safe framework for practice.

Where respondents were specific, three main perspectives were said to underpin practice – either singly, or (often) in combination:

- the *ecological* approach, which allows for a holistic assessment of an individual in their environment;

- the *developmental* approach (sometimes combined with *attachment* theory), which sets an assessment of the child in the context of normal child development across a range of dimensions. This approach was widely identified with the "Orange Book" style of assessment; and

- a *systems* approach to family therapy, which focuses on the whole family and interactions within it.

The first and third of these approaches were combined, for example in the practice of the specialist centres in London (Marlborough) and Birmingham (Woodside); and staff were clear about the ways in which the combined approaches informed their work.

Does it matter whether people undertaking the assessment of children and families are familiar with the theoretical basis for their work? The evidence collected by Inspectors suggests the following conclusions:

Clarity and system in the application of theory to practice is important in every case, even where an "eclectic approach" is appropriate. Data can be (and sometimes are) collected without a theoretical framework, but cannot be analysed without one.

Where assessment is the starting point for establishing a treatment plan, understanding the basis on which judgements are being made is important: where assessment in some way *incorporates* treatment, it is crucial. This point was especially relevant to some of the smaller units which had "therapeutic" goals in assessment which were not always tied to a clear theoretical framework.

Where assessments involved work with very troubled families, a clear, known framework based on theory and elaborated by experience and review is fundamental to good practice. (See, for example, the framework developed by Howe and associates (1998) at the University of East Anglia, which offers a developmental framework for information gathering, observation, analysis of needs and risks of significant harm, the formulation of aims and the deployment of services and treatment).

The two most sophisticated specialist units in the sample (8 and 9) were able to provide evidence of the place which theory played in their work. At the Marlborough Unit, staff were working within a systems-based framework for assessment; and in their ongoing treatment of some families, they might also deploy psycho-dynamic and learning theory. Behavioural therapy and sometimes complementary therapies might be used. Staff at the Marlborough are obviously appointed partly because of the professional background which they can contribute to the team: they also receive training within the Unit. It is unusual in the sample in offering family group therapy. The case files seen by the Inspector showed a level of good practice in assessment which is partly attributable to the coherence provided by the framework described here. Staff at Marlborough were also clear about the race, culture and gender factors which might contribute to the families' (and workers') experience. This clarity, which was found relatively rarely in the sample as a whole, will be discussed further in the next Chapter.

The Park Hospital Unit works within an ecological perspective. It has developed a clear conceptual framework for analysing the process of and potential for change in a family, as well as for assessing risk of significant harm, within a number of domains. The ecological approach is integrated with developmental factors which are seen as of "central importance" (Jones, 1996). The notion of maintaining "a child's eye view" of events is promoted as a way of keeping the interests of the child paramount: " – one of the easiest traps for therapists to fall into… is to forget temporarily that the purpose of the treatment is to improve the child's predicament; the adult's individual needs should come second..." (Jones, 1997). In their ongoing treatment of families, staff at the Park use a range of therapies including systemic family therapy, cognitive therapy, focal family therapy and psycho-analysis. The coherence and (related) effectiveness of the team are achieved by regular reviews of work in an atmosphere of mutual respect, and articulation of the basis of their practice in the publications of the Unit's leader.

6 Values

At almost every site, respondents were more easily able to describe the values which underpinned their work than the theoretical basis for it. Their personal philosophies, and the philosophy of their agencies were usually summed up in phrases like these:

- needs-led and child-centred;

- respect and empowerment;

- the dignity of the individual;

- openness, and partnership with families.

Clearly, there may be situations in which not all these aspirations are mutually reinforcing. It may, for example, be very difficult to be both child-centred and in partnership with parents simultaneously. Inspectors found that many of the agencies visited had explored some of the inevitable ambiguities of their work. This might well happen in the context of local debate about new procedures:

> Development of new procedures in Kensington and Chelsea (11) has involved the SSD in fundamental discussions about the nature of "needs" and "outcomes", and the functions of assessment.

> The project being undertaken in North Lincolnshire which is led by a team from the University of Leicester (4) has stimulated inter-agency debate about "good-enough parenting" in the context of developing an assessment tool for multi-agency use.

In the larger specialist units, issues like these would be explored in training and review sessions, and – in one case – by participating in debates in the academic literature. Perhaps the least capacity for debating and analysing the value base to their work was found among the smaller units. In some cases, these "inherited" a fully-formed philosophy from a parent organisation which they had neither the time nor the incentive to take apart. But this was not inevitable: Woodside, for example, had developed its own clear, coherent documents within the general framework of the policies established by the NSPCC.

Stating a philosophy, and putting it into practice are of course two different things. Inspectors found that – in general – the specialist units were effectively pursuing their ideals through the work they did with families. All of them seemed able to put principles of openness and partnership with parents into effect without losing their focus on the child, and an "ethos of respect" was discernible in the day-to-day work of staff. This was partly due to the fact that the role which they played in relation to the family was very different from that of statutory agencies; and this could occasionally cause conflicts with the purchasing agency. The same openness still seemed much more difficult to attain in some SSD settings. Inspectors found that one aspect of this related to the – often understandable – fear of violence which inhibited some social work staff in their work with families. Clearly, practice which is open and confident has its foundations in leadership, training, and management support, as well as clear and consistent procedures.

There was some evidence that the family centres which were often used by SSDs as partners in the assessment process had some of the characteristics of specialist units in the extent to which they were able to offer open communication to and relationships with families. A family centre operating in Kingston, for example, offered a needs-led service, which focused on practical, practicable outcomes. Staff operated in an open, honest way, and parents were given regular feedback. The possibility of collusion, or manipulation by parents was avoided by systematic supervision, monitoring and evaluation.

Equality of opportunity

One way in which commitment to equality of opportunity was demonstrated was the extent to which staff were aware of and owned the equal opportunities policy of their agency. Although there were exceptions, Inspectors found that this was a weak area for the sample as a whole. Some units had acquired a policy from a parent organisation, but there was little sign of it being known or implemented. Some SSDs had complete and *active* policies, or were in the process of developing one; but for others, the policy was – at best – just another piece of paper. Evidence of systems for monitoring equal opportunities policies was found in SSDs; less often, in the smaller specialist units.

The corollary of the existence of a coherent and known policy is of course that it should be followed through in practice. Some agencies would argue that the population which they serve is uniformly white; but this begs the question of the extent to which the service they provide is partly determining their clientele. The task of adapting the whole process of assessment and treatment of children and families to an ethnically and culturally diverse population was being tackled in at least some of the sites visited. Both the Woodside and Marlborough Units were particularly active in this area, and both could provide at least one clear example of where in the past a lack of understanding on the part of referring agencies had led to problems for families. The referring agencies had clear equal opportunities policies, but these were not put into practice – leading to agency neglect in one case, and conflict and delay over decisions in the other.

> At the Marlborough Unit in London, the commitment of the agency to providing a service which is relevant to all potential service users is reflected in practice. The Unit has worked hard to produce an ethnically-sensitive package of services, and has acquired a reputation with local, black families for fair and useful treatment. Developing an ethnically-mixed staff has been a high priority for recruitment, and of the 35 staff, 15 are from minority ethnic groups, with cultural and linguistic backgrounds appropriate to working with local families. A training scheme for minority ethnic therapists has been run in-house; and a Pakistani researcher is currently employed to investigate the impact of offering a culturally diverse service for referrals.

> Woodside works in the context of the NSPCC code of practice which puts equal opportunities at the heart of good, anti-oppressive practice. The racial and cultural identity of a child is seen as central to assessment and planning; in one case, for example, this led to the recommendation that a mixed-race child should live with her Asian parent and step-parent, rather than with white, racially prejudiced grandparents.

For many agencies, the issue of gender equality in recruitment is equally difficult. The only real evidence to suggest that these issues were understood and incorporated into practice was found at the Woodside Assessment Centre. At another unit, the wholly female staff were aware of the issues raised by employing men to work with young children, but had been unable to resolve them. Male applicants for vacancies were said to be ruled out by their "lack of experience of work with young children" – an ultimately self-fulfilling obstacle.

7 *Procedures*

All five of the SSDs visited in the course of the study were selected partly on the grounds of local procedures for assessment which were thought to be original and/or particularly effective. The five sites are Kingston upon Thames (**1**), Stockport (**2**), North Lincolnshire (**4**), Nottinghamshire (**5**) and Kensington and Chelsea (**11**). In three cases (**2, 4** and **11**), the procedures were still at the development stage. The paragraphs below summarize some of the key features of the procedures in all five sites.

Impetus for change/purpose

1	**2**	**4**	**5**	**11**
To build on existing procedures in the light of "Messages from Research", and experience.	To promote accessibility, equity and consistency; and minimise distinctions between assessments.	To devise assessment tool, related to LAC materials, reflecting standards for "good enough parenting".	To develop an integrated approach, and get away from process-led practice.	Stimulated by refocusing debate to develop needs-led approach.

Structure of assessment procedures

Kingston had developed a standard referral and assessment form, for use by social workers as a screening device leading on to any of the following:

- initial assessment, where intervention may be required;

- child in need assessment;

- child protection investigations;

- "safeguarding" assessment (where there is concern rather than proof of danger);

- a comprehensive (LAC) assessment.

A further assessment might be needed by disabled children.

The strengths of this approach were:

- generally *clear and specific* documents;

- documents *inter-connected*, and system flexible;

- some *prescription* in documents ensured that jobs were done;

- documents incorporated a useful casework planning sheet.

Discussions with staff, and scrutiny of case files suggested that some procedures involved repetition of information, and therefore increased the already bulky documentation; that the information collected was not always relevant, and that the standard of recording did not always match the standard of assessment. Questions were raised about whether the introduction of the notion of "safeguarding" as a type of assessment and as a level of priority could be confusing; and staff were also conscious of the need for more and better analysis of the information collected.

Stockport was in the process of implementing a simple procedure, backed up by clear guidance, for all work with children and families, (in which the SSD takes the lead). It incorporates the following elements:

- Service User Information Sheet, for use for all referrals requiring any action;

- initial assessment, for all cases requiring action beyond the duty officer – the form incorporates a genogram;

- core assessment – for all ongoing cases. This may lead on to:

- a comprehensive assessment.

The procedure for child protection cases is the same, but guidance puts "assessment of risk at the heart" of such cases.

The strengths of this approach appeared to be:

- *simplicity, clarity and coherence;*

- *child at the top of the agenda* in initial and all further assessments;

- the system *legitimises the initial assessment*, and makes sure that information about possible problems is found early.

Further development is needed to ensure that the procedures (and practice) incorporate work with other agencies.

North Lincolnshire SSD in conjunction with the Children's Joint Planning Locality Group have worked with a team from the University of Leicester and the local voluntary sector as well as local statutory agencies and Members to develop a simple assessment tool for all agencies, based on an agreed set of standards for "good-enough parenting". This was still in the development stage, but the basic structure was already clear. It offered a relatively brief form, incorporating instructions for use and definitions, which enabled any professional to record "mild", "moderate" or "serious" concerns about a child, within 6 domains (closely related to, but not identical with the 7 LAC domains) of need.

The strengths of the approach included:

- *simplicity, clarity, comprehensiveness;*

- based from the start in *joint work,* and uses multi-agency vocabulary and concepts;

- extensive *local consultation*, including parents and children;

- the tool is clearly *child-focused.*

Achieving local ownership has taken time, but is an important element in the development process which has produced the tool.

Nottinghamshire implemented the APIR framework, developed by consultants, in 1997. It was stimulated by the sense that a series of difficult cases had paralysed practice, and had created procedures which inhibited social workers from exercising their professional judgement. It had the following components:

- brief Level 1 assessment establishes basic information, summarized main issues, needs and risks; it may lead on to S.47 enquiries, and/or;

- a Level 2 assessment, incorporated an assessment plan, assessment of the family's circumstances, and assessment of the child using the 7 LAC domains. It may, in turn, lead on to;

- a comprehensive assessment.

The strengths of the approach are:

- components are *clear and well-structured*;

- it represents a systematic attempt to *"change the language"* of assessments, and develop an integrated approach;

- it incorporates a clear focus on the *needs of the child* (Section "C");

- it incorporates *clear thresholds* for moving between levels;

- it enables *analysis of needs and risks*.

Problems could arise with the system if the information it generates is thought by staff to be too long and cumbersome. Joint working has yet to be fully developed under this system.

In **Kensington and Chelsea SSD**, work stimulated by the Refocusing debate had led to the development of a new assessment and recording process. This involved:

- a screening level, involving taking referrals, recording basic details and arranging for immediate services; and

- a needs-led assessment, which was as detailed as necessary to reflect the complexity of the case. The assessment was based on a child development model and covered the needs of both children and of parents/carers. Where risk becomes paramount, the assessor could move to a parallel child protection process, in which risk issues were highlighted.

Assessments were recorded on a document-based computer system, which was designed to meet the needs of practitioners and appeared to be user-friendly. Assessments were carried out as appropriate by social workers or family centre workers. Joint working with education and health had yet to be developed. Potential strengths of the system appeared to be:

●   clarity (particularly when the assessment was under child protection procedures), and consistency with the community care assessment system;

●   a clear focus on needs and outcomes in assessment;

●   good file management on computer, and rapid retrieval of forms and documents (which were inter-connected) on each case; and

●   the potential for delivering aggregated information on needs, services and outcomes.

All of these initiatives offered insights into what makes a new, local system work. From their analysis of the documents, and discussions with staff and managers, Inspectors found:

●   greater acceptance and use of new procedures where the development of local ownership had been given high priority;

●   a widespread acceptance of a developmental approach to the assessment of children, which had useful implications for joint work;

●   a range of approaches which put children in need higher on the agenda;

●   an integrated use of family centres (1 and 5) which increased flexibility;

- interest in, and creative systems for training (1, 5 and 11); and

- a function for "champions" – an individual or group charged with maintaining momentum in implementation (1, 5 and 11).

Reporting instruments which maintained a balance between prescription and triggers for analysis were most useful. Bulk was a general problem: it could be alleviated by selective collection of information; summary sheets; and – to avoid repetition – the creation of a "core document", maintaining basic information on the case:

- procedures from a number of sites were compared by Inspectors with the criteria listed at the end of the previous section. There was, of course, considerable variation, but a few general points emerged. Firstly, ownership has not only to be created but *sustained*. It has to reach all parts of the organisation – all area teams, night staff – to be effective. A minority of agencies within the sample aimed to include families in this sense of ownership. The documentation in units tended to be less obviously complete (and bulky) than in some SSDs. The pros and cons of these sometimes "paper-light" systems will be considered below. Where extensive procedures existed, practice did not, of course, always bear out the rigour implied by the instructions, and staff working on designing systems were constantly having to weigh comprehensiveness against practicality;

- evidence collected by Inspectors suggested a further criterion: that procedures should relate in several different ways to the *reality* of both the family's situation and the possibility of improving it;

- firstly, in terms of the *level of assessment* implied by the facts of the case (the correct level was not invariably identified);

- secondly, by distilling the *key features* of the case, and seeing them clearly in the context of the family's history and present situation;

- thirdly, by identifying *capacity in terms of behaviour;* and

- fourthly, by looking at the past and present in terms of *the future* – what can really happen next?

Studies informing the Framework for the Assessment of Children in Need and their Families

Finally, Inspectors found that good procedures, while necessary, were not enough to produce good practice. Apart from factors like training and supervision, a culture of innovation and creativity was necessary to ensure the commitment of staff to the difficult process of change.

8 Experts

Specialist units were well represented in the study sample. They ranged from a small, voluntary organisation offering low level family support, to a state-of-the-art assessment and treatment service for children and families with multiple problems. The costs of using these facilities varied by a factor of at least 50. In some respects, they appeared to resemble each other – in their relatively (relative to SSDs) relaxed approach to paper and "bureaucracy", for example. But these similarities were superficial. Some units maintained a fairly paper-free environment by establishing a clear, theory-based ethos to which all staff subscribed and contributed. Close joint work ensured that methods were understood and reviewed. For a minority, the lack of paper reflected a general uncertainty about objectives, and about policies determined by parent organisations. But this is not to say that good work was the preserve of the expensive, sophisticated end of the scale: Inspectors found sound assessments and useful outcomes in some of the smaller units as well.

Who buys these services, and why? Dare et al (1990) have suggested that referrals are made to specialist agencies for one of three reasons, " – dysfunction in the referral agency's decision-making process, a need for education, or a wish for an alliance with a more powerful agency". The last of these factors rang true with respondents in some SSDs, who talked about units being able to lay hands on specialist information more easily, or about courts having more confidence in reports written by experts. A related point was that some social workers now felt that they had no function in working directly with young children – there was "always someone else" who could or should take the job on. Perceived obstacles to and problems with direct work with children included:

- the need to use a worker already known to the child;

- the lack of management expectation that social workers worked with children;

Studies informing the Framework for the Assessment of Children in Need and their Families

- lack of training and skills;

- the perception that small children cannot clearly express their feelings;

- gender and safety issues for male workers, and lack of guidelines about this; and

- resistance and sabotage from abusing parents.

Some respondents in units, on the other hand, took the view that it was their role to contribute to decisions which were too difficult or painful for social workers to take alone; and there were examples in the case-study material of families whose relationship with statutory agencies had reached the point where useful work could only be done in a fresh context. Referrals to specialist units were often made in the context of legal action, and might be made directly by the courts or Guardians *ad litem*. Where this happened, liaison with the "home" social worker was not always smooth.

Inspectors' visits to units raised a number of points:

- Is the increasing use of units creating a vicious circle in which both the courts and social workers themselves are losing confidence in the latters' capacities? Or are some units filling the gap while social workers acquire specialist skills? Or − more simply still − is their use just a function of heavy SSD workloads?

- Useful work is being undertaken by units, but they are not, of course, without problems. They frequently experience difficulties in securing the full co-operation of SSDs, and there were comments about missed meetings and slow responses to requests for information.

- The acquisition of specialist reports from psychiatrists, psychologists and even education staff caused significant problems for SSDs and units alike; but units are sometimes able to access these more easily, either through purchase or on site. Clear expectations between agencies about the functions of specialists, including time-scales, would improve the services offered to families.

- Only one Unit (Park Hospital) had the means to monitor the outcomes of the treatment they offered, by a postal trawl of families. Others – Westwood House, for example – aimed to offer some follow-up, practical and emotional support, which they contrasted with damage to families created by the abrupt withdrawal of packages of care.

It is important to distinguish between type and scale of unit. Arguably, the level of documentation required of a small unit offering observation rather than changes in behaviour should be relatively low. But some key documents were not always present.

Since units provide a service for other agencies, their costs were better known and available at most sites. But it is not easily possible to make a judgement about the relative cost-effectiveness of the units without more information about both costs and outcomes. However, allowing the child care capacity of its own staff to wither must always be an expensive option for SSDs.

The conclusion drawn from the site visits was that there was indeed an important specialist function which units could usefully perform. But this must be locked into SSDs overall strategies for assessment of children in need and SSDs case-load management, to avoid the danger that they may in time simply displace local authority social worker competence.

There is another sense in which "experts" are relevant to the assessment process. Both SSDs and units use people with specialist skills in specific roles: both Nottingham and Stockport SSDs, for example, used consultants in developing their new procedures, while Kingston commissioned a review of its recording system from an academic expert. Units too have employed consultants for specific purposes; but typically, they tend to include a range of expertise in their teams, with a wider network of specialists – psychologists for example – on call. Both models can be useful in supplementing the core skills needed in an assessment team.

9 Management

Management support is especially relevant to the implementation of new procedures, and this has already been touched on in Chapter 7. Briefly, Inspectors found that senior management leadership, in the sense of creating an atmosphere responsive to change, was essential to the process of *embedding* new systems. Sufficient management time had to be allowed for implementation: there were examples of new systems losing momentum when key management figures moved on. Once a procedure was in operation, the scrutiny of first line managers was crucial in ensuring that practice was consistent with policy. Social workers commented that Team Managers who provoked analysis and allowed staff the freedom to make judgements within a known framework were most appreciated. In Kingston SSD, for example, there was a management culture which encouraged creativity and initiative, which in turn enhanced the quality of assessments.

Costs

SSDs were in general unable to provide much information about how much their own assessments cost, so that no comparison could be made (by them or by the study) with the costs of specialist services. The units visited varied in terms of cost. In 1998 these were as follows:

- The Park Hospital Unit (8) charges (usually the Health Authority) £4096 for a two-week in-patient assessment. A Court report, follow-up at Child Protection conferences and so on are provided as needed, at additional cost.

- The Marlborough Unit (9) provides a non-residential comprehensive assessment for between £3500 and £5000. Packages vary, but could include, for example, a week of daily, family attendance at the Unit, plus outreach and school-based work for 4-6 weeks. The costs may be partly covered by Legal Aid, more often by the SSD.

- Westwood House (3) charges from £700 to £1600 per week per family for residential assessment, which is almost always met from the Child Care budget of the SSD. This covers court reports, conferences and similar tasks.

Units also vary, of course, in what they provide for the money, and an assessment of their relative value would require much more information than is summarized here. The principal finding of Inspectors, in relation to costs, is that the kind of management information which would enable SSDs to make informed judgements about how to use their child care resources was not available.

Training

Training has been mentioned throughout this report in a variety of contexts. It has been identified by SSDs as a vital component in their strategies for implementing new recording systems. Social workers have commented that the training they received did not equip them for work with children and families; and some new social workers, fresh from courses, were not familiar with the provisions of the Children Act 1989. The gaps identified between aspirations, philosophies, theories and policies on the one hand, and practice on the other have all suggested the need for further training. But of what kind?

> Kingston SSD had developed a new strategy for staff training, which incorporated training on assessment into a modular approach which focused on *core competencies*. Staff emphasized the importance of training which is *integrated* in to the process of implementing new initiatives; and which offers *practical* as well as theoretical help.

> In Nottingham, the implementation of the new system was backed up by a systematic programme of training. The staff development unit at Nottinghamshire SSD is planning to work with practice teachers to ensure students on placements get experience of assessment work, with the aim of increasing assessment and analysis skills amongst newly qualified practitioners.

> An initial approach in Kensington and Chelsea, which focused on new forms and IT systems, was found to be unsuccessful. A review of the project led to an emphasis on the assessment process itself, and found that a combination of training and coaching was necessary to successful implementation. Training is provided on needs-led assessment and negotiating outcomes with the family,

followed by training on the IT system. This is reinforced by on-site coaching from an experienced social worker seconded to support practitioners.

In some of the specialist units – Woodside and Marlborough, for example – there was a commitment to continuing training, as well as a more general encouragement to the acquisition of knowledge through peer support, reflection and review.

Monitoring and evaluation

Most of the SSDs which were implementing new systems had built in some system of monitoring and evaluation. The criteria used, in general, related to managerial efficiency – acceptance and understanding by social work staff, throughput of cases and so on. In effect, they were implementing a process, and undertaking a process evaluation. The *impact* of the process, on outcomes for children and families, is more difficult to measure and few Departments in this sample were confident that they had the means to do so. One exception was Kensington and Chelsea, where the routine monitoring of the process, although not fully developed, was ultimately intended to deliver information about outcomes.

The specialist units were almost all equally unable to provide any information about outcomes. Some commented that they received no further information about the families they saw from referring agencies, once the assessment was complete. For most of them, the "outcome" is the acceptance by the referring agency of their plan; and broadly, they measure their success in terms of take-up, attendance (by hard-to-reach families) and "consumer" (agency and sometimes family) satisfaction. Again, there was one exception in the sample: the Park Hospital (8) is able to provide data on the number of families going home together after treatment; and more importantly, is planning a follow-up study of outcomes for users.

10 Footnote

The study produced several different kinds of evidence:

- about the links between theory, philosophy, policy and practice;

- about effective and practical ways of coping with what one Inspector called the "paper mountain" generated by assessment;

- about useful ways to differentiate between the roles of statutory and voluntary, and general purpose and "specialist" agencies;

- about the use of experts to supplement the skills present in an agency team; and

- about the ways in which innovation can be supported by management, and an ethos of creativity and reflection, supported by clear processes for implementation and monitoring.

One important conclusion reached by Inspectors is that, among the sample, there is very little systematic information about outcomes on which a judgement about the relative quality of assessment systems could be based. All other observations should therefore be seen in the light of this caveat. But they have been able, on the basis of the material they collected to identify factors likely to make for a more effective system, and these have been summarized here.

A second, fundamental conclusion is that procedures and practice which encourage the full involvement of children and put them firmly at the centre of the assessment process are being developed in a range of settings. The aspirations to put children first, to operate openly and without oppression, to respect families and be aware of issues relating to race, gender and culture – all of these can be supported by the kinds of techniques found in the agencies studied.

Thirdly, no single blueprint for an assessment system was found which would be useful everywhere. Central to the effectiveness of any agency was the way it linked into local, professional and community networks; and Inspectors found that the process of developing a local system was often crucial to local ownership and understanding.

But while systems can and should be locally-tailored, the currently variable use of terminology is not helpful to the development of consistent practice. Clear terminology, which could be understood beyond the local SSD boundaries and enable comparison with practice elsewhere, was clearly desirable and not always found.

Finally, access to specialist resources, including specialist assessments and reports was found almost everywhere to be causing problems, and diminishing the quality of the service offered to children and their families. Clarifying inter-agency expectations – in particular about the role of Child and Adolescent Mental Health Services – and building these into the Children's Services Planning process would help to provide a coherent basis for future funding and development.

Many other questions have been raised by the visits, and some remain unanswered. What kind of training will be most appropriate to fit the social workers of the future for their role in child and family support? How can the widespread uncertainty about the social worker's role in direct work with young children be resolved? How can the existing gaps in management information – about the relative costs of different assessment services, or their relative success in terms of long-term outcomes for children and families – be filled? This study formed part of a wider Departmental review of the assessment process, and was designed to observe and distil some of the approaches which a range of agencies are developing to cope with the dilemmas discussed here. Their views, procedures and practice are offered as contributions to a continuing debate.

Appendix 1
SSI Study Team

Anne Mercer (Lead – Social Services Inspector, Department of Health)
Jenny Gray (Social Services Inspector, Department of Health)
Helen Jones (Social Services Inspector, Department of Health)
Lesley Moore (Social Services Inspector, Department of Health)
Peter Munro (Social Services Inspector, Department of Health)
Ruth Newton (Social Services Inspector, Department of Health)
Peter Stone (Social Services Inspector, Department of Health)

Diana Robbins (Consultant)

Appendix 2

Study Method

The aim of the study was to examine innovation in assessment, focusing on policy, management and practice. Inspectors followed a common methodology in work with eleven sites, representing a range of settings in which social workers might take part in assessing children and families.

Each site visit typically comprised two days of documentary analysis, case-study analysis, observation and interviews.

Documents which were studied included examples of as many as possible from the following list. Analysis of the documents covered the characteristics of the agency, the values and theoretical basis for its work, and the quality of the documents themselves.

Document list

Policies, procedures and guidance relating to assessment work, including ACPC procedures.

Assessment forms/*proformas* for recording, including any parts of the form which were to be copied to the parent/child.

Leaflets, booklets and other public information about the assessment process.

Service level agreements, contracts, costings for assessment work commissioned from other agencies.

Staffing structures in relation to assessments, including assessments of disabled children.

Joint working protocols for agencies undertaking joint assessments.

Training courses, and content on assessment.

Procedures for assessing disabled children.

Three case files were reviewed in each setting. The focus of the review was the relationship of the recording system used to the accuracy of the final assessment. Where possible, cases involving a preliminary screening assessment, an initial assessment, and a comprehensive assessment were studied. Information about the referral, the assessment process, the outcome, plans for future work and recording tools was collected.

The study incorporated some time for **observation** of the reception process and setting for new referrals. In addition, in some settings Inspectors had the opportunity to observe other assessments as they were taking place.

Interviews: at each site, a series of semi-structured interviews were completed with senior managers, managers, and key workers. The last of these were the key workers who had been involved in the cases already studied by Inspectors. The aims of the interviews were to elicit information about:

- strategic issues on assessment (senior managers);

- policy and procedures (managers);

- practice in specific cases (key workers).

Every stage of the study was prepared according to a **common format**. Inspectors were provided with detailed schedules which served as structures for interviews and checklists for observation, as well as frameworks for their reports. This meant that – despite the complexity of the area of study – different sites and different kinds of practice could be compared in some detail.

Reports by Inspectors were analysed and synthesized by a consultant. Drafts of this **final report** were reflected back to the study team on three occasions for their amendment and validation. It was, finally, sent to all the agencies which participated in the study for their comments on its factual accuracy.

Appendix 3
Study Sites

Kingston–upon–Thames SSD (pilot)

Stockport SSD

Westwood House, Peterborough Family Care, Northampton

North Lincolnshire SSD (Home–Start/Leicester University)

Nottinghamshire SSD

Woodside Assessment Centre, Birmingham

Bewick Family Centre, Gateshead

Park Hospital, Oxford

Marlborough Unit, London

Broxtowe Family Centre, Nottingham

Kensington and Chelsea SSD, London.

References

Dare, Goldberg and Walinets (1990) quoted in Wheeler, J., Bone, D. and Smith, J. (1998) "Whole Day Assessments: a team approach to complex multi-problem families", *Clinical Child Psychology and Psychiatry*, 3, 2.

Howe, D. *et al.* (1998) "Developmental Attachment Theory, Child Maltreatment and Family Support: a practice and assessment model", Working Paper, School of Social Work UEA.

Jones, D. (1996) "Management of the sexually abused child", *Advances in Psychiatric Treatment*, 2, 39-45.

Jones, D. (1997) "Treatment of the child and the family where child abuse or neglect has occurred", in R Helfer, R Kempe and R Krugman (eds.) *The Battered Child*, Chicago University Press.

Seden, J. (1998): *Literature Review: Contributing to the Development Framework for Needs-Led Assessment of Children and Families*, Report to the Department of Health.

Study D

Analysis of child care inspection findings (1992-1997) on assessment

Clare Pont

Study D: Contents

1 *Introduction*

Background

A trawl of child care inspection findings on assessment was commissioned by the Department of Health in November 1997 and are summarised here. The primary objective of the report was to identify from the child care inspection reports key messages for practitioners, first line and middle or senior managers and policy makers in relation to the tasks of assessment. The findings informed the development of the Framework for the Assessment of Children in Need and their Families (Department of Health et al, 2000).

A summary of the findings are collated under the headings listed below:

- Policies and Procedures for Assessment;

- Compliance with Legislation, Guidance and Policies (National and Local);

- Quantity and Quality of Initial Assessment;

- Quantity and Quality of Comprehensive Assessment;

- Supervision and Management Responsibilities for Assessment;

- Competencies of Staff to Undertake Task and Training Requirements;

- Joint Assessments;

- Resourcing Issues.

The key features which are needed to construct a good assessment system and underpin good practice were identified and are listed below. They take account of the various stages of assessment at the time the work was undertaken, and link assessment to planning.

Methodology

The trawl was carried out by way of a detailed analysis of a wide range of reports of SSI child care inspections which were undertaken between 1992 and 1997.

The types of inspections covered were:	Number of Individual Reports	Number of Overviews
Child Protection	37	
Local Authority Adoption Services	13	
Voluntary Adoption Services	1	
Local Authority Fostering Services Reports	9	4
Children in Need	7	1
Disabled Children	7	3
Local Authority and Independent Child Care Centres Under 8s	6	1
Assessment, Planning and Decision Making, Family Support Services	8	1
Residential Child Care	15	1

The list of key features set out in the next sections summarise the information extracted from the different types of inspection reports.

Although few of the inspections concentrated specifically on the task of assessment, decision making and planning the features that emerged were remarkably consistent.

2 Polices and Procedures for Assessment

Summary of key features

Key messages for Senior and Middle Managers and Policy Makers

- Policy, procedures and practice guidance are clearly differentiated;

- Policies and procedures contain a clear requirement that services are provided on the basis of a needs assessment;

- Policies and procedures on assessment incorporate racial and cultural factors;

- Guidance on assessment contains clear timescales for completion;

- Services provided by the SSD are clearly set out and understood by staff.

3 Compliance with Legislation, Guidance and Policies

Summary of key features

Key Messages for Senior and Middle Managers

- Policies and procedures require rigorous and repeated implementation training for staff;

- Policies and procedures are reviewed regularly to ensure that they reflect best practice;

- Monitoring systems that are clearly understood and applied by managers and staff;

- Procedures set out very clear requirements for recording which includes the basis on which decisions about services are taken;

- The provision of services is regularly reviewed to ensure that services are provided appropriately and fairly;

- Service users views are sought on a regular basis in order to monitor whether they were offered the services they required.

4 *Quantity and Quality of Initial Assessment*

Summary of key features

Key Messages for Senior and Middle Managers

- A clear distinction needs to be drawn between S. 17 referrals and S.47 enquiries;

- All cases are re-assessed and appropriately re-routed when necessary;

- Service priorities are based on accurate management information about referrals;

- Self-referrals can provide the clearest source of information about services user's need, wishes and views. This source of information needs to be utilised more effectively;

- A high percentage of 'emergencies' often results from ineffective referral taking and assessment rather than being an emergency;

Key Messages for Social Workers

- Sufficient information is taken at point of referral to enable effective decision making;

- Recording of referral data is full and accurate;

- Lack of clarity about services provided locally blocks service delivery for some would be users;

- Accurate information is given to those who self-refer on how to access services and on services provided.

5 Quantity and Quality of Comprehensive Assessment

Summary of key features

Key Messages for Senior and Middle Managers

- Best practice was noted where assessments were carried out by confident, experienced and well trained social workers;

- Assessments carried out in Family Centres were more detailed and enjoyed service user confidence;

- A range of specialist staff to be provided for undertaking effective assessments, e.g, in Family Centres, Specialist Teams, Dedicated Workers;

- Inter-agency protocols, staff support and understanding the roles of other professionals are essential elements of a comprehensive assessment;

- Assessment work requires rigorous management oversight and monitoring of compliance with policy and procedure;

- Social workers require specialist supervision and consultation in carrying out complex assessments.

Key Messages for Social Workers Undertaking a Comprehensive Assessment

- Suitable training is essential;

- Assessment work needs to be carefully planned;

- Adequate time needs to be allocated to complete the work with targets set for completion;

- Clear and accurate recording is an essential component of a good assessment;

- Assessment reports require a recognisable structure, should demonstrate the decision making process and always be shared with the relevant parties;

- Involvement of staff with specialist skills, including working with children;

- The views of children, families and carers are clearly identified in the report;

- Assessment reports must demonstrate the decision making process which led to the specific plan;

- Plans which follow an assessment of need to have clear objectives, timescales, details about the purpose of interventions and the services to be provided and by whom.

6 Supervision and Management Responsibilities for Assessment

Summary of key features

Key Messages for Senior and Middle Managers

- The quality of supervision is related to the skills, competence and experience of individual supervisors;

- Supervisors' training needs in providing quality supervision on assessment work is identified;

- The quality of assessment work is routinely monitored by senior managers;

- Clear expectations as to how cases are prioritised, allocated and monitored;

- The quality of recording and adherence to policy and procedural guidelines is closely monitored and endorsed in writing by the supervisor;

- Management information systems are reviewed to ensure that they provide accurate and usable information;

- Quality standards for assessment work are established;

- Roles of senior practitioners/internal consultants, vis a vis supervisors, are clearly established.

Key Messages for Line Managers/Supervisors

- Supervision should be:

- Regular;

- Well structured;

- Free from interruptions;

- Monitored for compliance with policy and procedures;

- Address issues of competence;

- Used to ensure decisions are recorded on case files and that recording is up to date and complies with local procedures.

7 Competencies of Staff to Undertake Task and Training Requirements

Summary of key features

Key Messages for Senior and Middle Managers

- Best practice in assessment was achieved by social workers who were confident, well qualified, received skills based training and specialist supervision;

- In-house competency assessment, comprising written and verbal tests, is a requirement for social workers undertaking complex assessment work;

- Training strategies which follow detailed training needs analysis are essential;

- Staff competency is monitored through appraisal;

- Specialist training in all levels and types of assessment work is essential.

8 *Joint Assessments*

Summary of key features

Key Messages for Policy Makers, Senior and Middle Managers

Effective Joint Assessment work is dependent upon:

- The establishment of joint policies, protocols and frameworks for undertaking assessment work;

- Procedures which set out each agency's responsibilities and tasks;

- Rigorous management oversight;

- Establishment of mutual priorities for getting the work done;

Key Messages for Practitioners

- A consistent approach to undertaking joint assessments;

- Careful integration of information from other agencies into the assessment, planning and decision making process.

9 Resource Issues

Summary of Key Features

Key Messages for Policy Makers, Senior and Middle Managers

Efficient assessments are dependent on:

- Clear service level agreements;

- Agreement about access to services;

- Service provision based on identified need;

- Recruitment of staff from black and ethnic minority groups qualified to undertake assessment work;

- Well co-ordinated services.

The most commonly noted shortfalls in available resources in undertaking assessment work were in the following areas:

- Educational psychology;

- Psychiatric assessment;

- Assessment and treatment for a wide range of abusers;

- Assessment services for black and ethnic minority groups;

- Lack of competence and skills in SSD staff;

- Inadequate management information systems to aid service planning;

- Repeated restructuring which leads to loss of skilled workers.